WRITING NATURAL HISTORY Dialogues with Authors

Barry Lopez and Edward O. Wilson
Robert Finch and Terry Tempest Williams
Gary Paul Nabhan and Ann Zwinger
Paul Brooks and Edward Lueders

Edited by Edward Lueders

D0188226

University of Utah Press
Salt Lake City
1989

Material from *Biophilia* used by Edward O. Wilson in Dialogue One copyright © 1984 by The President and Fellows of Harvard College

Library of Congress Cataloging-in-Publication Data

Writing natural history : dialogues with authors / edited by Edward
    Lueders.
        p.   cm.
    ISBN 0-87480-323-3
    1. Natural history — Authorship.   2. Natural history literature.
    I. Lueders, Edward G., 1923–
    QH14.W75   1989
    808'.066508 — dc19   89-4764
                                                              CIP

Dedicated to

Edward Abbey, 1927–1989

CONTENTS

PREFACE

Each year the University of Utah appoints a member of its faculty to the rank of University Professor. This honor enables the recipient to undertake projects that will enhance the cause of liberal education within the curriculum and beyond. As University Professor for 1987–88, I was thus able to arrange a series of four public programs, held on the first four Mondays in February, 1988, entitled "Writing Natural History: Dialogues with Authors."

This series brought together four pairs of eminent authors in the expanding fields of natural history. Although they knew and respected one another's work, only one pair, Gary Nabhan and Ann Zwinger, had met previously. At noon, each pair gave a joint reading from their work at the Utah Museum of Natural History, a co-sponsor of the project. In the afternoon they met with student writers. In the evening, they engaged in the informal public dialogues that comprise this volume. In between there was plenty of convivial, eager offstage conversation.

The participating authors were selected not only for their eminence, but also for the variety of their perspectives on natural history and their stylistic diversity as celebrated writers for a broad reading audience. They included both men and women; writers from the east, the south, the midwest, and the west; younger writers, older writers, and writers in mid-career. The first three dialogues brought together scientists who write with uncommon skill and imagination and creative writers who are avid observers of the natural world. The fourth dialogue paired authors with long careers in the publishing and teaching of nature writing.

The dialogues took place on the uncurtained platform stage of the University's 400-seat Fine Arts Auditorium. The setting consisted simply of a living-room-size carpet with comfortable chairs for the participants. At the side of the chairs were end tables for books, papers, water pitchers and glasses, and the single prop that Terry Tempest Williams surprised us with each week — a different plant or modest flower arrangement keyed to the particular pair of authors and their work.

Although in a few instances the authors drew from printed material or began from casual notes, the dialogues were purposely unstructured and impromptu. I was present as moderator, but the direction came easily from the mutual concerns and individual experience of the two authors.

The unique nature of the occasion and the exchanges between the writers — and their audience — depended on the spontaneity of extemporaneous conversation. Although some editing was necessary to assure coherence on the page, we have tried to maintain in print the vitality of the spoken dialogues. The lively sense of being on the edge of each speaker's utterance is an important part of these published dialogues — as it was on the occasions themselves.

I am indebted to a great many persons — above all to Barry Lopez, E. O. Wilson, Terry Tempest Williams, Robert Finch, Gary Nabhan, Ann Zwinger, and Paul Brooks for their good faith and readiness to collaborate in the project, which was made possible in part by a grant from the Utah Endowment for the Humanities, a state-based affiliate of the National Endowment for the Humanities. Dean L. Jackson Newell and Associate Dean Karen Spear of the Liberal Education Program of the University of Utah lent support and assistance at all times, as did Cynthia Buckingham of the Utah Endowment for the Humanities and the staff of the Utah Museum of Natural History. I am especially appreciative of the skill and care of Susan Browning in transcribing these dialogues from the audiotapes and for her role in preparing the manuscript for publication.

Edward Lueders
Salt Lake City, Utah

THE CONTINUITIES
OF NATURE WRITING

The nature essay must be one of the most stable genres in literature. Looking at the earliest samples—the Rev. Gilbert White's *A
Natural History of Selborne* (1789), say, or William Bartram's *Travels*
(1791)—and then coming forward through Thoreau and Muir and
Burroughs and on to such writers of our own century as Donald
Culross Peattie, Rachel Carson, and Barry Lopez, one is struck by
the absolute durability of certain subject matters, themes, and affirma-
tions. Even the stylistic idiom doesn't seem to have undergone any
very dramatic transformation: one can read Bartram today, for example, far more comfortably and familiarly than his near-contemporary,
the novelist Charles Brockden Brown. Nature literature appears to
have been so firmly rooted in its basic methods and allegiances that
currents of intellectual fashion and even deep philosophical change,
in the culture at large, seem hardly to have disturbed it. There are
no sharply defined "periods," no reactions between movements such
as the romantic disapproval of overly dry reason, or the realists'
later scorn for the excesses of romanticism—those well-known turns
in the thought of the past two centuries. More profoundly, the literature of natural history did not fall into existential terror or despair
at sight of the naturalistic world first clearly described by the biologists Darwin and Wallace. As the scholar Robert Richardson has
pointed out, the implications of evolution seem to have been quite
clear to Henry David Thoreau, for the earliest example, who read
The Origin of Species within a few weeks of its publication. Thoreau
took down several pages of notes on the book, and not only was he
not revolutionized, he was quick to see how his own field work in
seed dispersal and plant geography might conceivably make a con-

tribution to evolutionary studies and to the overcoming of static, creationist ideas of nature. The Concord naturalist may have been particularly receptive to evolutionary theory because so much of his own experience in the woods and fields had been transcendental — that is, of a kind to break down the cultural orthodoxy that things have hard borders: "I go and come with a strange liberty in Nature, a part of herself."

Thoreau had been walking along the stony shore of Walden Pond on a cool and cloudy summer evening when, for no particular reason that he could single out, the "environment," as we call it, and the "self," as we call it, became numinously coparticipant: "Sympathy with the fluttering alder and poplar leaves almost takes away my breath. . . . " This is the lyric core of the nature essay. It is the experienceable aspect of ecology.

John Muir, too, readily accepted evolutionary theory in the broad sense, writing of man as having "flowed down through other forms of being"; though he was constitutionally opposed to the concept of struggle or "survival of the fittest," Muir saw clearly into evolutionary time. His freedom to imagine transhuman ages, and thus his insights into glacial history in the Sierra Nevada, were apparently furthered by powerful epiphanic experiences. For long periods of solitary mountain rambling during the glacier study, Muir's journal records an intensely receptive consciousness: "The sun shines not on us, but in us. The rivers flow not past, but through us, thrilling, tingling, vibrating every fiber and cell of the substance of our bodies. . . . "

Delight need not be overtly transcendental, of course. But there is an edge of meaning to any awed description of nature; what is being called forth is, in effect, the world before the Fall, before any sense of alienation. The sight of birds in abundance, in particular, seems reliably to have evoked the former earth in its wholeness, and the paradisal, human capacity for wonder. William Bartram in his *Travels* wrote,

> It is a pleasing sight at times of high winds and heavy thunder storms to observe the numerous squadrons of these Spanish curlews (White ibises) driving to and fro, turning and tacking about, high up in the air, when by their various evolutions in the different and opposite currents of the wind high up in the clouds, their silvery white plumage gleams and sparkles like the brightest crystal,

reflecting the sunbeams that dart upon them between the dark clouds.

Two long, checkered centuries after the *Travels,* and a continent away from Bartram's green Florida, Barry Lopez in *Crossing Open Ground* marveled at a similar scene, this one created by snow geese at a refuge in northern California:

> I remember watching a large flock rise one morning from a plowed field about a mile distant. I had been watching clouds, the soft, buoyant, wind-blown edges of immaculate cumulus. The birds rose against much darker clouds to the east. There was something vaguely ominous in this apparition, as if the earth had opened and poured them forth, like a wind, a blizzard, which unfurled across the horizon above the dark soil, becoming wider and higher in the sky than my field of vision could encompass, great swirling currents of birds in a rattling of wings, one fluid recurved sweep of 10,000 passing through the open spaces in another, counterflying flock, while beyond them lattice after lattice passed like sliding walls, until in the whole sky you lost your depth of field and felt as though you were looking up from the floor of the ocean through shoals of fish.

Powerful aesthetic experience like this may be what keys a nature writer into the creative world of source, but in the process of composition that original impetus is almost always joined with respect for scientific fact. A distinguishing mark of the nature essay — and this has been true from the beginnings of the genre onward — is precisely the attempt to harmonize fact knowledge and emotional knowledge. Annie Dillard wrote a good deal of the evocative *Pilgrim At Tinker Creek,* apparently, in a library carrel, with over a thousand note cards on natural history at hand. Ann Zwinger's books have a great deal of time in the field behind them, but she too is an assiduous user of libraries. Gary Nabhan, whose writing can evoke a strongly poetic sense of desert spaces, is a professional botanist. To go back a bit, the later journals of Thoreau, which some literary critics have groused about for their scientific content, are actually one of the better demonstrations we have of the wholeness of outlook that characterizes the best nature writing. Quite early in his career, in 1842, Thoreau had written, "Let us not underrate the value of a fact; it will one day flower in a truth," and that utterance hits the tone of the nature essay perfectly. The literature of natural history often utterly transcends the notorious "two cultures" dichotomy. For an immediate instance, the dialogue in this volume between E. O. Wilson and Barry Lopez demonstrates again that science and aesthetic-emotional-intuitive knowledge not only coexist in nature writing, but conspire to suggest something greater, as it were, than the sum of the parts.

But for all the nature essay's perhaps placid-seeming consistency over time, there is genuine revolution in it. Even at its most genteel (and nature writing is polite letters), it is subtly, inherently subversive. Seeing, simply seeing, destroys divisions; for however brief a time, it restores health. The nature essay re-enters the world that we, in our "progress," attempt to leave behind. At a wilderness camp in Georgia, deep in his travels into the interior, William Bartram declared himself and his companions to be "far removed from the seats of strife," and "strangers to envy, malice, and rapine." How different the oil camps in the far north described by Barry Lopez in *Arctic Dreams* (some of them "little different from the environment of a small state prison, down to the existence of racial cliques"), yet how similar the basic criticism. Much of the nature essay's charge comes from this comparison of worlds. Its alliance is always with the organic, personal, and sacred. William Bartram never succeeded in the business world. He lived out his life, after the great, dazzling travels, on the edge of Philadelphia, dressed in leather, puttering around barefoot in the famous garden his father had made, keeping lists of birds, helping out younger naturalists. His story might be seen as a commentary on us all, for at the root of our pathological bigness may be only the littleness of ego. And what can the nature essay teach us about *that*? Fitting in, reciprocity, quietness? It is not irrelevant, perhaps, that Henry Thoreau was both a nature writer and a political philosopher—that is, a student of the adjustment of ego to reality—and that Barry Lopez, in a recent note, has speculated that the literature of nature might "provide the foundation for a reorganization of American political thought." What seems to be involved is an entire psychic reorientation. "A way to do this is to pay attention to what occurs in a land not touched by human schemes, where an original order prevails," Lopez writes in *Arctic Dreams*.

So the nature writer is working on a new-old myth, as Robert Finch says in his dialogue here with Terry Tempest Williams. "Storying the landscape," in Finch's phrase, means restoring relation-

ship, and in this, perhaps, might lie our redemption, both ecological and political. An old American theme, redemption, as old as
Bradford and Winthrop. But now, perhaps, we begin to see it as not
strictly a human drama; everything is hitched to everything else, as
John Muir said. At the height of the experience of the wild, Muir
affirmed, "no petty personal hope or experience has room to be."

Perhaps the sense of place begins here, in this adjustment of
the ego. Famously mobile, we have five centuries of exploration and
expansion for an identity. Even now, when all the land is owned by
someone or other, we continue to drive from place to place, raising
dust. But the Rev. Mr. White stayed put in Selborne, and so did
Henry Thoreau in his town, pretty much. If you are alive to connection, Selborne and Concord are enough. One of the strongest
moments in these dialogues is Terry Tempest Williams's avowal of
belonging to the Great Basin environment, both natural and human.
She recounts a memory of crawling across a path of grass as an
infant, going toward her mother probably, and the feel of the grass
becoming a kind of imprinting, a seal of membership which is per-
manent because it is, in truth, cellular. Our deeper identity, the
literature of nature reminds us, goes back infinitely farther than our
known and written history. Dolores LaChapelle tells us that at
Bollingen, as an older man, Carl Jung "kept it all very simple,
without electricity, chopping his own wood for fuel and pumping
his water by hand." In this placid circumstance, Jung wrote in his
autobiography, "Thoughts rise to the surface which reach back into
the centuries, and accordingly anticipate a remote future. At times I
feel as if I am spread out over the landscape and inside things. . . . "

The extraordinary, mythic attractiveness of home ground, of
making the gift of self to it, of becoming more capable simply to
stand still and see and hear; of learning what other lives occupy and
interweave with each other on the very same ground: all this is a
radical reversal of our usual bluster. But we know better than we
have done, and have so known, at some level, since at least the time
when William Bartram stood meditatively in the garden, his feet
touching the earth. We keep reminding ourselves. The literature of
nature, as the concluding dialogue between Paul Brooks and Edward
Lueders shows, has always been more than just nostalgic. It has
enlarged perception, inspired legislation, even kept hope alive. There
are three editions of so antique a book as Bartram's *Travels* — 1791! —
currently in print, and how many of Thoreau and Muir? Our appe-

tite remains sharp. Perhaps this is true most obviously for Americans, who in a kind of genetic memory have held what F. Scott Fitzgerald called the "fresh green breast of the new world" clearly in mind. Perhaps we will never forget it. Every night of this series of dialogues, people began coming to the hall as early as an hour before time. As the place filled, an unmistakable keenness of attention grew. People's voices had eventfulness in them, and their glances traveled frequently to the still-empty stage. In the middle of a well-paved city, in a university auditorium moreover, sitting in padded, metal-framed chairs, hearing the little preliminary snaps and clicks of audio equipment, we waited for words inspired by a world entirely different, yet as familiar as our bones.

Thomas J. Lyon

Dialogue One

ECOLOGY AND THE HUMAN IMAGINATION

Barry Lopez and
Edward O. Wilson

February 1, 1988

BARRY LOPEZ, recipient of the 1986 American Book Award for *Arctic Dreams*, has contributed widely to an awareness of landscape and the imagination. He is noted for a prose style that is elegant and exact. Mr. Lopez received the John Burroughs Medal for distinguished nature writing for *Of Wolves and Men* (1978) and a Guggenheim Fellowship for 1988, the year *Crossing Open Ground*, his book of essays, appeared. His collections of fiction include *Desert Notes*, *River Notes*, and *Winter Count*.

EDWARD O. WILSON, Baird Professor of Science at Harvard University, ignited a blaze of controversy with *Sociobiology: The New Synthesis* (1975), which maintains that the biological principles underlying the structure of animal societies are applicable to the social behavior of humans. Among Mr. Wilson's awards are the National Medal of Science and the Pulitzer Prize for General Nonfiction. He is also the author of *On Human Nature*, *The Insect Societies*, and *Biophilia*.

LUEDERS: Good evening. It is my privilege to welcome you to this series of dialogues on writing natural history under the auspices of the Liberal Education Council of the University of Utah, with the co-sponsorship of the Utah Museum of Natural History.

My name is Ed Lueders. The names of our two authors, Barry Lopez and Edward O. Wilson, you know or you wouldn't be here in such numbers, sitting so avidly waiting for their conversation that will ensue. I have asked that their conversation be, in effect, a dialogue with one another. But they have been puzzling, I know, about how they might best get under way with the dialogue. The suggestion I am going to make is that they revert to what they wanted to say as they thought ahead to this evening together. I am going to ask first Professor Wilson, Baird Professor of Science at Harvard University, to tell us about his perspectives on science and the humanities as they come to us through writing natural history.

WILSON: Well, it's everybody's favorite subject whenever they bring up interdisciplinary studies, and I feel that in the exposition of natural history and the translation of science through that conduit, we have an extraordinary opportunity to bring about that grail of the academic community in a convergence of science and the humanities. I have prepared some notes I would like to follow briefly— mercifully briefly. Don't look too worried, Ed. [laughter] I should have opened the attaché case, you know, and brought out a . . .

LUEDERS: I notice it comes from a yellow legal pad, without which none of us can operate.

WILSON: As soon as I picked it up and started to read it, I could have accidentally fumbled and had it fall all over. [laughter] But it is just a couple of pages, and I thought it would be helpful. This is a last gesture that might look formal before we get started on this subject.

Shelley wrote in his essay "A Defense of Poetry"—it was an amazingly modern insight—that one of the artist's tasks is, to quote him, "to absorb the new knowledge of science and assimilate it to human needs, color it with human passions, and transform it into the blood and bone of human nature." No scientist would write that, but lots of scientists think it. And that isn't easy at all, of course, because in part, particularly in the domain of natural history, we are faced with a dilemma symbolized by the dominant metaphor in the relation between science and nature, which is the machine in the garden. The machine is a technological advance instructed by scientific knowledge on which our modern and very comfortable civilization exists. But the machine tears apart and degrades the natural environment in which the human species evolved over two million years. And to turn to *it* is something that I believe we innately do for spiritual peace, for some sense of the ancient genetic heritage that we have. Human history is being increasingly translated into the precise language and often strange idioms of evolutionary biology, geology, and other disciplines of science. At another level, nature writing, I would like to suggest, although my distinguished colleagues may differ on this point, faces the same crisis of the machine in the garden. The question is, How can precision, analysis, and specialized vocabulary, the hallmarks of the scientific idiom, be married to the rich metaphorical language of literary expression, which is the ancient ancestral mode of expression? How can increasingly scientific natural history maintain art? And, finally, how can art climb up on the top of scientific knowledge in order to survey the world and expand our field of vision?

So tonight you have two practitioners. One is a creative writer who masters those portions of science relevant to his vision, and the other a scientist who tries to pass scientific knowledge through the prisms of literary expression. A creative writer who is exact, and a scientist who, when freed from the editorial policy of the *Proceedings of the National Academy of Sciences* and other scientific journals, tries to write like a poet. I suggested the resolution to this dilemma in the following way in the book *Biophilia.* And, if you will bear with me just another moment longer, I would like to read this because it puts it as precisely as I can, and I think it is germane to the subject of the writing of natural history. We are confronting in this passage one of the most beautiful and spectacular organisms on earth, the Emperor of Germany bird of paradise (I love that—I mean, even before you see the bird: the *Emperor of Germany bird of paradise*) on New Guinea. And, as I have written:

The jewel of the setting in the Sarawaget Mountains, which I was able to explore biologically as a young scientist, is the male Emperor of Germany bird of paradise, arguably the most beautiful bird in the world, certainly one of the twenty or so most striking in appearance. By moving quietly along secondary trails you can glimpse one in a lichen-encrusted branch near the treetops. Its head is shaped like that of a crow—no surprise because the birds of paradise and crows have a close common lineage—but there the outward resemblance to any ordinary bird ends. The crown and upper breast of the bird are metallic oil-green and shine in the sunlight. The back is glossy yellow, the wings and tail a deep reddish maroon. Tufts of ivory-white plumes sprout from the flanks and sides of the breast, turning lacy in texture toward the tips. The plume rectrices continue on as wire-like appendages past the breast and tail for a distance equal to the full length of the bird. The bill is blue-gray, the eyes clear amber, the claws brown and black.

This improbable spectacle on the Huon Peninsula of New Guinea has been fashioned by millions of generations of natural selection in which males competed and females made choices, and the accouterments of display were driven to a visual extreme. But this is only one event, seen in physiological time and thought about at a single level of causation. Beneath its plumed surface, the Emperor of Germany bird of paradise possesses an architecture culminating an ancient history, with details exceeding those that can be imagined from the naturalist's simple daylight record of color and dance.

Consider one such bird for a moment in the analytic manner, as an object of scientific research. Encoded within its chromosomes is the developmental program that led with finality to a male bird of paradise. The completed nervous system is a structure of fiber tracts more complicated than any existing computer, and as challenging as all the rain forests of New Guinea surveyed and seen on foot. A microscopic study will someday permit us to trace the events that culminate in the electric commands carried by the efferent neurons to the skeletal-muscular system and reproduce, in part, the dance of the courting male. And so on down to the cell. Down to the molecule. Biology sweeping the full range of space and time. Discoveries constantly made increase the sense of wonder at every step of research. By altering the scale of perception to the micrometer

and millisecond, the biologist parallels the trek of the naturalist
across the Huon Peninsula. He looks out from his own version of
the mountain crest. His spirit of adventure, as well as personal history of hardship, misdirection, and triumph, are fundamentally the
same.

Described in this way, it will have occurred to you, the bird of
paradise may seem to have been turned into a metaphor of what
humanists dislike most about science: that it reduces nature and is
insensitive to art, that scientists are conquistadors who melt down
the Inca gold. But bear with me for a moment. Science isn't just
analytic; it is also synthetic. It uses artlike intuition and imagery.
In its early stages, individual behavior can be analyzed to the level
of genes and neurosensory cells, whereupon the phenomena have
indeed been mechanically reduced. In the synthetic phase, though,
even the most elementary activity of these biological units creates
rich and subtle patterns at the level of organism and society. The
outer qualities of the Emperor of Germany bird of paradise, its
plumes, dance, and daily life, are functional traits open to a deeper
understanding through the exact description of their constituent
parts. They can be redefined as holistic properties that alter our
perception and emotion in surprising and pleasant ways, and a new
natural history emerges.

There will come a time when the bird of paradise is reconsti-
tuted by the synthesis of all the hard-won analytic information. The
mind, bearing a newfound power, will journey back to the familiar
world of seconds and centimeters. Once again the naturalists will
begin to take form and step through the moss-covered trails. Once
again the glittering plumage takes form and is viewed at a distance
through a network of leaves and mist. Then we see the bright eye
open, the head swivel, the wings spread wide. But the familiar
motions are viewed across a far greater range of cause and effect.
The species is understood more completely; misleading illusions
have given way to light and wisdom of a greater degree. One turn
of the cycle of the intellect is then complete. The excitement of the
scientist's search for the true material nature of the species recedes,
I would claim, to be replaced in part by the more enduring responses
of the hunter and the poet.

What are those ancient responses? That is the pivotal question. The full answer can be given only through a combined idiom
of science and the humanities, whereby the investigation turns back

into itself. The human being, like the bird of paradise, awaits our examination in the analytic-synthetic manner. As always by honored tradition, feeling and myth can be viewed at a distance through physiological time, idiosyncratically, in the manner of traditional art. But they can also be penetrated more deeply than was ever possible in the pre-scientific age, to their physical basis in the processes of mental development, the brain structure, and indeed the genes themselves. It may even be possible to trace them back through time past cultural history to the evolutionary origins of human nature. With each new phase of synthesis to emerge from biological inquiry, the humanities will expand their reach and capability. In symmetric fashion, with each redirection of the humanities, science will add new dimensions to human biology.

And that is the way I would like to suggest the fiery circle of science and the humanities could be closed and creativity in the two branches of learning might converge. And, again, as I say, the logical conduit for much of that effort would be through natural history and nature writing of the kind that may well be emerging into its twenty-first-century form.

And now, Dr. Lueders, it will be impromptu for the rest of the evening.

LUEDERS: I see that the paper went back in the coat pocket. It's almost a position statement — a position paper. Barry: equal time. [laughter] I don't want to set this up as a debate rather than a dialogue, but you'll want equal time, I believe.

LOPEZ: Actually, some of the things that you said, Ed, anticipate some questions that I would like to see us address this evening. One of my favorite ideas is the antiphony of birds, the calling of one bird to another. When I was thinking ahead about this evening, I thought of this because we come from different disciplines and yet before us is the same dark forest. And we form a community that, for diverse reasons, wants to understand the forest. So I thought this evening was like an antiphony of sorts, of calling back and forth to each other the best that we could offer from our experience.

There are three issues at least that I hoped we would touch on. I apologize in a way because they are all very difficult, but it seems an opportunity to address them and I would like to try to do that.

The first is an ethical issue for me. It is that, as a writer, I am dependent on scientific inquiry for information. If I am going to write coherently — about polar bears, for example — I am dependent upon the scientists who work with polar bears for solid information of a certain sort. And yet I am troubled by this because of the ways in which we approach animals as scientists. If I take the long view in talking to cultures other than my own outside of North America, I see animals essentially in a defensive position in the world — in defense of their homes and in defense of their cultures, if you will. The question that this raises for me is the right of privacy as we are to understand it with respect to other organisms. We are intensely curious, and I am troubled sometimes myself — for I would put myself at the center of this as well — by the ramifications of my inquiry, my invasion of privacy of the world that animals have. We have changed in the past ten thousand years or so from groups of people who were surrounded by animals. We now have small enclaves of animals surrounded by people. I feel an intense desire to know something of those other cultures, of those other nations. But I have questions because my culture is so clever, so adept, so powerful, so colonial that the animals don't have a chance to say that they don't wish to speak or have their privacy invaded. So that ethical question of invading the privacy of those other nations is one issue.

The second is an epistemological issue. It has to do with the way we organize the way we see the world. How do we as scientists and as humanists organize the world? One of the things I've discovered as a writer when I travel is — for example, when I am traveling in the Arctic and talking to archeologists, anthropologists, biologists — they all see the world in a different way. Part of the delight of being in that position is hearing people express with great passion and in an unguarded way the delight they have in seeing an aspect of the world that is to them like a piece of the face of God. It is utterly mesmerizing, and it is that to which they have devoted their lives. But, when I listen to men and women speak like that and then move off some weeks later to another camp or have an opportunity to talk to somebody else passing through the same region, I realize that they see something completely different. What you learn from this experience is that the dark forest is in certain ways unfathomable. There is no end to the kind of inquiry that can be made. And I lament sometimes that there are those who lack a capacity for metaphor. They don't talk to each other, and so they don't have the

benefit of each other's insights. Or they get stuck in their own metaphor, if you will, as a reality and don't see that they can help each
other in this inquiry that binds people like ourselves together. So
this issue arises for me: what do we know? how do we know? how
do we organize our knowledge? I mention this in part to remind
myself always about my own tendencies, because of my cultural
upbringing, because of the way I was educated, to see things in the
light of my traditions and my beliefs.

Western philosophy is organized, according to one way of thinking, into five divisions: metaphysics, epistemology, logic, aesthetics,
and ethics. And each of them, if you will allow me to generalize,
poses a different question. Metaphysics asks the question, what is
real? And the central question in epistemology, I think, is, what
can be known? And in aesthetics it is, what is beautiful? In ethics it
would be the question of how one should behave. And in logic it is,
what is the trustworthy pattern? What is a pattern that you can put
your trust in?

The first time that this occurred to me was when I was traveling with Eskimo people in Alaska. There is a certain way, both
because you are white and because you are of the dominant culture,
that you must allow yourself to be made the butt of jokes in a culture like that. It is the proper thing to do. [laughter] And they are
expert in the probing of your misgivings about your own culture.
They can make life very miserable for you. If you talk to anyone
who has spent time living with native cultures in North America,
they will, I think, tell you the same thing — that sooner or later you
are driven to a point in which you feel a fierce sense of the dignity
of your own culture. In my experience with native peoples, the true
exchange does not begin until you've reached that plateau. They are
less and less interested in you the more and more interested you are
in being like them — because they know you can never be like them.
What they wish is that you would express, with the integrity of your
own positions in a discussion or in the way you live, the best of what
your culture represents. Then there is something to talk about. I
became very defensive in my mind one day walking along thinking,
"We must have done *something* right." [laughter] And one of the
things that came to mind was these divisions of philosophy.

So I posed those questions to myself, and I would think about
them while I was traveling with these men. I would wonder, "What
do they think is the trustworthy pattern here? How do they put this

particular pattern of weather, this density of ringed seals, these how-old polar bear prints in the snow—how do they put this together and develop a pattern that is trustworthy upon which one can base a particular action that one is going to take?" I proceeded in ignorance. They were my tutors. I could with the proper analytic arrogance have said, "I can figure this out, too." But I don't know that I would have put it together the same way they did. And then, of course, there's this marvelous question of what is beautiful. Is that man's heart taken as much by the way this light floats on this water—like molten manganese—as mine is? And, if it is, what does that mean? The central question of how we organize this information—how we organize the world we see—is of interest to me. It not only seems dangerous to say that all cultures organize it the same way, but also very dangerous to say all people organize it the same way. It speaks against something that is sacred to both of us, which is this issue of biological diversity.

The third question is harder to phrase. I want to do it with the utmost respect because I am going to use some words of yours, Ed, that help me illuminate the problem. One of the marvelous things about story, about what story does, is that it creates both a surface reality and a reality in parallel, which allows you to appreciate something both directly and indirectly, some aspect of life obliquely. Story has a way of disarming or dismantling the flow of time by its use of tense; it creates an environment where the mind can rest; it can move about and come to feel coherent or healed. I talk sometimes about what I call the literature of hope, by which I mean a literature that can bring hope to bear on the things that confound us, the meretricious business of day-to-day living. How can we surmount those kinds of incidents, that kind of day-to-day living? How can we get beyond it? One of the ways is with a literature of hope.

So I think of this kind of parallelism, where a story powerfully illuminates something happening in our culture or out on the land by both setting it out straightforwardly and by evoking or capturing some less obvious meaning. In the same way, some of you who know the history of photography will recall how Alfred Stieglitz—I guess around 1915 or so, probably a little earlier—began working on his series of photographs he called "equivalents." He was photographing clouds, and the clouds in some way were equivalent to certain human emotions. I think in literature—you have to correct

me if I'm wrong; it's been a long time since I thought about this—
this is the idea of the objective correlative.

When I first began traveling with native people and trying to
listen to the way they talked about animals, I would occasionally
find—this is true in any discipline—that something new would suddenly fall into place. One of those things fell into place for me one
time when this man said that animals and people were parallel cultures. He saw the culture of bears or the culture of wolves or the
culture of any animal developing in parallel to human culture. I
began thinking about these parallel systems, where, if the two cultures were traveling side by side, you could make inquiries across
the chasm. That's what the shaman does. To my way of thinking,
that is also what a scientist does, and the writer in another way.
They reach across some dangerous chasm, where they are at great
risk, to inquire of a parallel culture, to ponder another order, for
how it might illuminate some part of their own culture.

Now the ideas that I wanted to refer to, which are yours, Ed,
are your feelings that natural selection—that is to say, genetic chance
and environmental necessity—made man, not God. And a related
idea, that man is a "physiochemical mechanism" rather than a "ves-
sel of a mystic life force." The question that I have is: why can't it
be both? If we are able to learn so much from these parallel structures and if we know from the arts that it is this extraordinary
thing, the metaphor, that functions in dance, that functions in paint-
ing, that functions in sculpture, that functions in literature to allow
us to grasp something esoteric in parallel—if we know this is true in
the arts and we know that we are excited by that, isn't it possible for
us to say that, rather than man being exclusively the creation of
God or exclusively the result of natural selection, isn't it possible to
say that it is both? That these are parallel ways of understanding?
That, rather than being mutually exclusive, they are mutually informative?

So those three questions: This general idea of how so much of
what we comprehend is through the parallel of metaphor. This epistemological question of how we organize the world as scientists and
humanists, how we organize the phenomena that we see. And this
admittedly difficult question of propriety when it comes to our curiosity about organisms other than ourselves. [pause] A couple of
light matters . . . [laughter]

WILSON: Barry, as you were talking, I kept thinking to myself, "These questions . . . I hope what he is talking about are the great questions for humanity generally to be considering. I hope he doesn't mean they're questions *I* am supposed to answer." [more laughter]

LOPEZ: No, no, no, no. We're both in the same dark forest. I just want to know if you see anything up ahead that I need to know about. [still more laughter]

WILSON: Let me tell you that I, like you, began my life with a rather strong religious background. I think that our ways of viewing things do differ. Where we have arrived at the present time, these two positions do differ. And let me see if I can express in a concrete and clear manner the position I am in now. As a kind of trial journey, I've moved to an entirely materialistic, scientific, humanistic position from which to consider the human condition. Somehow I believe that we can explain humanity entirely in a manner in congruence with physical-chemical laws, most of which are known at the present time, that it is possible to account for human origins up to and including the most advanced mental properties as the outcome of evolution that is preceded primarily by natural selection acting in a blind manner on self-assembling, giant replicating molecules. A blind manner. Blind in the sense of having no external guiding force and without reference in the realms of ethical precepts, without reference to any absolute rules external to the human species. This is a philosophical conjecture. It is powered or legitimized by the enormous advances of science in the last hundred years, rolling back frontier after frontier in the explanation of the world that seemed so mysterious to us as recently as just a hundred years ago. It withers somewhat and grinds to a halt in the mud and intense cold of the explanation of the human mind and of the spiritual qualities that you describe. Will we ever make it all the way? Is our mission going too slow? It is a philosophical position that probably only a minority of scientists and philosophers take; but, to put it another way, let us see how high we can fly until the sun melts the wax in our wings. It is not a dogmatic position. And it has the great advantage of producing explanatory power that could reach into all of those questions you just raised.

First of all, in the realms of philosophy that you described, it is possible that we could understand human epistemology as a series of distinct forms of information processing in the *Umwelt* that characterizes the human species as opposed to all other imaginable intelligent species. And, thus, our ways of perceiving truth could be viewed as products of our idiosyncratic genetic history — not as some direct perception that the human species has on absolute truth, but in a background of comparative evaluation of what is possible in the ways of seeing the world and of knowing truth that would allow us to come closer to a perception of all those possibilities and, therefore, in some sense, come closer to a view of absolute truth. And in aesthetics the same. Why do we regard certain things as aesthetic and pleasing and not others? Why do we regard figures with fifteen to twenty turns in them — that degree of complexity — as being aesthetically the most pleasing of all possible degrees of complexity? Well, we know that it damps those alpha waves in the EEG. Maximally, between fifteen and twenty turns — sixty percent redundancy. The human brain is built that way. It's not thirty or forty. It's not one hundred. It's not ten. It's between fifteen and twenty. And for that reason, probably, we pick out pictographs and ideograms and frieze design and grill design and abstract art of about that level of complexity. You can see what this can lead to. It can lead us to understand human aesthetics in terms of the product of genetic evolution without degrading it. We can come to understand how it might have come about. And in the realm of ethics. Why do we believe that some things must be done, are sacred, and other things are not so sacred and to be avoided? Why do we avoid incest, for example? We understand the basis of why we avoid incest, but I won't go into that. And so on through several categories of behavior. This knowledge is troubling in a way. It would be tremendously illuminating to somehow transform philosophy into the scientific study of human nature, to make ethical philosophy, for example, an applied science, to be guided by what Bertrand Russell said in a careless moment: that science is what we know and philosophy is what we do not know. [laughter]

But it leads to the doubts, and I think this brings us to the first and second of your three questions — how far do we have a right to intrude? I think you meant privacy in a more metaphorical way — the privacy of animals, of the living world. Do we really want to have searchlights rigged at twenty-meter intervals throughout the dark forest and a label on every one of the trees in that forest, cored for tree rings at three-year intervals? Do we want to live in a garden in which we know every leaf and twig and where it came from and its history? I rather doubt it. I don't think the human brain is built that way. I think we have to have a mystery and a sense of constant outward searching. And do we really want to understand, to the greatest depth, all of our idiosyncratic artistic impulses and so on? These are questions I can't answer, but I think they have the deepest philosophical import. And I believe that they represent a great seismic zone between science and the humanities that is going to come more and more to prominence. Our perception of the zone is enhanced by the tremendous ethical dilemmas being produced by deeper and deeper biochemical and molecular biological knowledge, which leads in turn to the control of all life, including human life.

But to conclude and return us to natural history and nature writing, the joy of it is that we will not in our lifetime and in any conceivable manner that we are capable of now plumb to the depths of life and understand it all. There are endless Magellanic voyages to be conducted around and around. Let me give you some figures. I know you know them already, but let me put this rhetorically. [turning to the audience] Barry and I have been talking all day, and he didn't hit me with any of this until now. [laughter] But we covered a lot of the ground leading up to it, discussing how we have not explored the whole world and why natural history is still very much in an early stage and why we are turning back to natural history.

By my latest estimation — I just did this for the National Academy of Sciences — there are 1,394,000 species of organisms of all kinds, including plants, animals, and microorganisms that have been described and given a scientific name. Most people who work on this subject believe that the actual figure on earth is somewhere between three and five million. There are upon the abyssal plains of the deep sea an estimated one million species of organisms, mostly unknown. There are in the treetops of the tropical forests, covering seven percent of this planet's land surface, an estimated thirty million species of insects alone, by one estimate, only a minute fraction of which have been explored in any sense. In the last thirty years, approximately twenty-five percent of all the reptiles known have been discovered and described. An entire new genus of reptiles is discovered and described somewhere in the world every six months, on the average. This is due to the expanding exploration of the world.

At the National Geographic Society centennial last week, a theme that was struck early on was that we have completed the exploration of the world and now the National Geographic Society must turn to such things as how to equilibrate humanity with the world in order to maintain a healthy and sustained social system. And I demur from all that. I say that we have just begun to explore the world. It is still possible for any individual to go on the equivalent of a nineteenth-century expedition to a valley in Ecuador or a peak in New Guinea and find new species of butterflies, to go to islands that have been virtually unexplored for whole sections of the living world. Recently, borings 250 meters down in the soil brought up previously unknown species of bacteria living on organic material drifting slowly down through all those layers of soil. And once we have discovered all of these and other species, if we ever do, then there is the endless voyage of working them out. So I don't think the dark forest will ever be fully explored, and the materialist's dream — the scientific-humanistic dream, to be more precise — of going to the bottom of it all remains only something that is, I think, best described as a philosophical position. Ultimate knowledge might be an abstract possibility but not in the detailed, emotional mode of natural history.

LUEDERS: May I raise a question from the standpoint of both reader and writer which I think may help to aim these weighty matters toward our common ground here? Because for a moment there, Ed, it was as if I heard you reading a page written by Barry Lopez, even though the figures, even though the information clearly came from your special background. But the eloquence, the elegance of what you were saying, as a matter of language, had that same sort of effect I experience when I read Barry's books. The common ground here is what I am curious about in asking this question. There is at the moment, unless my seismograph is out of adjustment, somewhat of an Earth movement — not only in the political sense, not only in that sense that exponents of global conservation are active among us, but among writers as well, among creative writers; and I am privileged to be talking to two of the most expressive and, I think, the most respected. What is its source in our society? Can you put your finger on it or do you have hopes, perhaps, to express? What is it that is responsible for the creative writing going on nowadays by many hands that is capturing an audience for books of what I would call creative nonfiction in the fields of natural history? Barry . . . ?

LOPEZ: Hmm . . . It's so pretentious in a way for me to even try to think about it. I think you can say some things in general about this kind of work. It is distinguished for me, first of all, as a kind of writing by the capitulation of various authors to a vision larger than their own. It seems to me that the people whom I read who are writing the best kind of natural history see something larger than their own universe, and, in that sense, it is an antidote to solipsism. To me, one of the greatest dangers in politics and in science and probably in other fields is this danger of a solipsistic universe — one that is entirely shut off from the universe that was *not* created and manipulated and changed to fit the fancies of one culture or another. I think people intuitively respond to that notion. They know that to have a universe entirely created by human beings is fundamentally insane. And the great danger in philosophy or whatever field you want to bring up, is living in a closed universe where all references are to oneself, to one's own way of seeing the world — and one is shut off. Natural history has served for forty thousand years at least — it's as old as the history of coherent narrative, as old as the history of the interaction of people with landscape — as a reminder of the breadth of the universe and the inability of the individual mind to encompass what is known or what can be known. So I think part of the attraction, part of what I recognize in this kind of writing, is a group of men and women whose vision is larger than their own artistic visions, for one, and whose vision of the universe is larger than the culture from which they come, the gender from which they write, the race from which they speak, the cultural history from which they emerge.

In my limited experience with other cultures in other countries, I find a tremendous sense of identification. I am thinking about a meeting I had with a group of writers at the International Writers Workshop at the University of Iowa, talking mostly to men and women who are novelists and poets and having them say, "You know, in our novels we address in a very direct way totalitarian themes." Take, for example, J. M. Coetzee's book, *Waiting for the*

Barbarians. Then one of the men said, "But, you know, you and these other American writers are addressing the same questions: totalitarianism, prejudice, dignity." What this makes me think is that part of the reason for turning to natural history writing is because it is written from a point of view that takes in a larger world than the world of just the writer. It brings us back to the traditional position of the storyteller in a community, which is not to be the wise person, the person who speaks from his own wisdom, but to create an atmosphere in which the wisdom inherent in the world becomes apparent. So you turn to natural history as a kind of writing that's not just about polar bears, or some other kind of animal, or plants or birds. It's about the fundamental issues of life.

The way I read American writing at the moment, these large important themes that ask "What are we doing in the world?" — these questions that I carry around and you carry around in another way, these things that we wrestle with as individual men, these questions that need to be addressed and which people are interested in having addressed, I think, *are* being addressed by natural history writers. They have been abandoned by fiction writers to some extent. At least when I look at letters that come to me or to my writer friends, this theme is reiterated constantly. They say, "I don't care so much about wolves or I don't care so much about this animal or that place in the world, but what you said about these things clarifies what I am trying to think about in the world in which I live, not just my little bailiwick and my ideas in my specific discipline, but in what I am trying to consider as a human being, what I'm trying to be as a human being. And to finish this, I think of the point you make, Ed, in *On Human Nature* about the relative speed of change — the rate of change — in Darwinian evolution as opposed to the rate of change in Lamarckian evolution with regard to human culture: the idea that human culture just expands out there in the distance, and if it gets too far off in the wrong direction, biological evolution reels it back in. It has this kind of constraining effect. One of the questions that I ask myself is why so many natural history writers are so attentive to cultures other than their own, whether they are attentive to Navajo culture or to Inuit culture or to Kalahari people, or whatever. And the answer that I keep coming to is that these cultures, if you remove the tendency to make a condescending judgment, are holding on to things that, whatever the basis for them, are fundamental to the spiritual and intellectual and physical health of human beings on the planet. So it is natural that natural history writers would go back to this older form, which is to tell a story about the universe outside the human universe that helps us understand what is going on within ourselves and how we are to behave. Also, I think that this is a literature that is so obviously a part of American literature. In the literatures of the world, I think this is something that American writers are offering to other cultures.

WILSON: After a scary initial detour through philosophy, I think Barry is bringing us back to the main subject. [laughter]

LOPEZ: Yeah. I was.

LUEDERS: With a little help from his friends. [more laughter]

WILSON: I'd like to build upon that, then, and hopefully bring us all the way back home.

LOPEZ: I hope I didn't go off too far.

WILSON: No. Actually, your questions and your inquiry were necessary prologue, I think. We had to have the setting, because it's fundamental.

Another way of putting what you were saying is as follows: We are preoccupied — that is, scholars in the humanities are preoccupied — with the last five or so thousand years of history, largely cultural in nature. But the human species was put together by two million years of history, from the first *Homo*. Most of that history is genetic. It had to do with the way that the human brain evolved — a 3.2-fold increase in the cerebral cortex alone, an astonishing growth. That's biological. And the way we think, what we can smell, what we can sense, the bonding that we make — the things that are the commonalities of human nature — are the result of that genetic history, which tends to be totally ignored by scholars in the humanities. And to understand that genetic history and, so to speak, the ultimate causes of human behavior is to address these fundamental questions, which, as you correctly point out, have been largely abandoned by novelists and many scholars in the humanities who remain focused on very relatively narrow, often discursive themes such as hermeneutics or deconstruction and the like. I don't want to get into that slippery slope, but I just wanted to mention this in passing—the *why* questions that used to be the domain of religion and the humanities are now solidly within the domain of the natural sciences. They include: What is the meaning of human life? Where did it come from? Why must we die? What is the meaning of senescence? Why are we programmed to die at around seventy years? What is the meaning of sex? Why are there certain forms of bonding and not others? And so on. These are the key issues that have to do with the essence of human nature, and they bring us, I think, in closer juxtaposition with explanations of the natural world, as you point out. Because to the extent that we have the conceit of separating ourselves from the remainder of the organic world from which we came—and not too darn many years ago—to the extent that we have the conceit of allying ourselves with some nebulously defined supernatural force or to say that in some manner yet unspecified we are tracking a set of ethical lodestars upon which we find it extremely difficult to agree and thus separate ourselves from nature and from the natural world, I think we are in deep trouble.

So this, then, is the special role of natural history writing—to incorporate the best of science in order to re-examine the natural world and the humanities' place within it in the scientific mode but through the prisms of literary expression.

And why do we need those prisms of literary expression? Because it will not do to have the literature—literature generally, and certainly all the writings about humanity—translated into the language of, shall we say, the *Journal of Biochemistry and Molecular Biology* along the lines of, "the average distance between the deoxyribose molecules is fifteen angstroms." That factual information has to some way be translated into forms that mean something for daily human existence, for the rules of thumb by which we live, and, above all, by the mode of storytelling. And this brings us back to natural history writing. Natural history writers are storytellers. Scientists are storytellers. Scientists live and die by their ability to depart from the tribe and go out into an unknown domain and bring back, like a carcass newly speared, some discovery or new fact or theoretical insight and lay it in front of the tribe; and then they all gather and dance around it. [laughter] Symposia are held in the National Academy of Sciences and prizes are given. [more laughter] There is fundamentally no difference from a paleolithic campsite celebration. The scientists tell the story, and the natural history writer's—the humanistic scholar's—one great function is to now translate it into the rhythms and the idioms of storytelling. And why do we need that? We go back again to the genetic history of humanity. For unknown thousands of years the brain was expanding by genetic evolution, in part because of the palaver and increasingly extended and complex storytelling that was told around the fire. The preliterate culture of humanity, as in the epic poem-tellers of some cultures still existing, gave tales of the history of the tribe and of great events that were recited, often over a period of days. And the storyteller has always had this central role in societies of translating that information in forms that played upon the great mythic themes and used the rhythms and the openings, the prologues, the body, the conclusion, the closures that make up literature. So the factual information that we get and the new metaphors created out of science somehow have to be translated into the language of the storyteller—by film, by speech, by literature, by any means that will make it meaningful and powerful for the human mind.

There's another compelling reason. I have to take the opportunity here to throw in conservation because this is a compelling issue of our time. Those species that we were talking about earlier are going extinct. I don't want to go into detail, but I will tell you this: because of the destruction of the tropical forests alone, at the rate of about one percent per year of standing cover—about one hundred thousand square kilometers per year of forest going down, probably almost irreversibly—that alone is destined at the present rate in the next fifty years to reduce the number of species on earth by twenty-five percent. It's the most since the end of the age of dinosaurs sixty-five million years ago. This is not speculation. It's what almost all scientists working in this field believe. We now have a sense that we are bringing life to a close. I mean, we're destroying life; we're reducing that natural world out there in an irreversible way. And I think that there is a sense of crisis here that is going to enliven and raise in magnitude of importance natural history writing of the new scientific form. I know for sure it is beginning to energize science. Right at the present time the biodiversity crisis is having an effect in the major scientific organizations. The National Science Foundation's National Science Board is having meetings on it right now on how to improve research in this area. Some of the major foundations, like the MacArthur and Pugh, are much more active now in looking at it to see what can be done. It is going to become a major issue of our time, scientifically and in public policy, particularly because of its occurrence in the third world where most of the population growth and habitat destruction continues. So for reasons quite external to the issues we have been talking about, I think we are going to find natural history coming on center stage. The biodiversity crisis will be another impelling force behind the clearer expression of the discoveries of evolutionary biology and natural history through creative writing.

LOPEZ: I think about something else, too. This gets off somewhat into a literary area, but not so far we can't get back. My sense of the men and women I know who write about these subjects is that they are a fairly congenial group of people. The human ego comes into this business all the time. I mean you have your own way of thinking and your own way of writing. You try to be deferential, but anyone who is writing is writing, in a sense, out of an extraordinary ego. It's an act of ego. It's a remarkable thing. And it can be preyed upon by the apparatus for celebrityism in our culture. So you create this curious situation where a group of people are writing about something that they understand fundamentally is larger than themselves, is more important than themselves—but in order to do it, it is an act of ego. And then along come the newspapers and other groups of people who create celebrities and, in some sense, sow contention. This is a general statement, but if you were to ask somebody who knows about what kinds of feelings American poets have toward each other, they would not be congenial. I don't mean to disparage that group of people or to condescend to them at all. There are certain attitudes that help define groups of writers, and it so happens—for whatever reason—that American poets are not generous toward each other.

Several months ago I read a draft of an introduction to an anthology written by Steve Trimble, who lives here in Salt Lake. He had gone around and talked to a number of writers of natural history. He is a man of great courtesy, and so I think a lot of people were very frank and easy in talking to him. One of the things he discovered, which struck home to me, was this deference that is shown by natural history writers toward each other—their mutual support and their regard for each others' work, which is genuine, and their affection, if you will, for each other. And I felt that sense of identification as soon as we met, that we were embarked on some similar process that was larger than the best either one of us could do in the world, being in service to something larger than ourselves. I think readers respond to that.

I think readers understand that our civilization is obviously having some extraordinary effect on the world. The upper atmosphere has our signature all over it at the moment. And the ozone hole in Antarctica, you know, is something to be deeply concerned about, along with the loss of biological diversity, the loss of species, desertification, the destruction of the rain forests. These issues, which so many people try to politicize, transcend politics. These are the fundamental issues of life. If we don't straighten these things out it is not going to make a bloody bit of difference whether you vote Republican or Democrat or whatever. But I think increasingly around the world there is this group of men and women who are in touch with each other — both scientists who are researching in certain areas to develop a body of knowledge that is dependable and informative and a group of writers and film makers and photographers who are trying to create a story that can be told that will make clear, not only from a journalistic point of view but from the point of view of the storyteller, from a literary point of view, from a point of view that fully entertains the mind, that these are crucial issues. They are issues around which one's individual reputation and one's desire to be well known simply aren't pertinent anymore. These issues are far too important to have those kinds of motives in the foreground. So often when I look at natural history work, I am made comfortable by it because it seems to me to be presented by people who, in addition to having their own vision about the way the world is put together — which may or may not speak to your frame of mind — have a sense of something going on that is more important than they are or than their culture is.

And here is an irony. The United States is supposed to be, or fancies itself to be, the best informed group of people in the world, and I think that's simply not true. Other cultures are more highly informed than we are, not only because they make it their business to be informed but because they live in an atmosphere in which it's necessary to know certain things. They are not the manufacturers of weapons. They are not one of the superpowers. Therefore, they are in a position and of a frame of mind to want to know a lot of things about how their lives are going to be affected. I find the issues that we would call "conservation issues" or "environmental issues"

addressed with tremendous passion and integrity and insight outside of North America. It's remarkable to me that we don't know
this about other countries. When I was with that group of foreign
writers at the University of Iowa, I expressed to a man from Costa
Rica my self-consciousness about being included in an international
group of literary writers because I work principally in this mode of
nonfiction. His response was that nonfiction is a form that we would
expect to develop in America before it would develop in any other
country because it's the form now proper to addressing some of
these very important issues. That was a great comfort to me. It
announced the currency of the things that I was struggling with, the
things that I was trying to clarify in my own mind: What is a dignified response to the land? What is it historically? What can one
learn about it by traveling with Inuit people? How does one establish a dignified relationship? (Which is what my question about the
invasion of privacy is.) How does one go about that? And I find
much help from cultures other than my own, as I did from native
people.

    I had the opportunity about three weeks ago to sit down in
Wellington in New Zealand and talk with the minister of disarma-
ment about New Zealand's policy against allowing ships carrying
nuclear weapons to enter their harbors. As this discussion went on,
I was thinking that, historically, nations influenced each other primarily along two avenues. One was economics and the other was
military force and the threat of military invasion or some kind of
military pressure. And here is this small country in the South Pacific,
and this man is saying to me (and he's my age, and that is the age
that matured in Vietnam), "You know, we really don't take our
direction any more from London. For better or worse, we are a
nation of white people in the South Pacific. Our neighbors are the
people of Fiji. Our neighbors are the people of the Solomon Islands.
And it is these people with whom we wish to associate ourselves
now. It is not primarily with the nations of the western world."
What he was saying is, "We are not moving toward neutrality or
toward an alliance with Khadafy or anything like that." What he
was saying is, "We have found our place in the world, and our place
in the world is in the South Pacific. We are an element in this ecosystem called the South Pacific. We are no longer an extension of
London." As he talked, I thought about these two avenues that historically had been used by nations to influence each other—eco-

nomics and the military. What he was articulating was a third avenue, the avenue of a dignified presentation of one's utter beliefs. In that moment there is no economics, there is no military. There is simply a human being among his or her culture standing up and saying, "We live with these elements of our ecosystem. These are the things we must do to survive as human beings." And I think that issue is underneath a lot of what natural history writing is all about.

I want to say one more thing. Once somebody came up to me and said, "Why do you go off and write about landscape or something like that? What is so attractive about it?" And I just answered with something off the top of my head, which later I meant to say. [laughter] It was one of those rare times. [more laughter] What I said was, "The natural world is a place where you can explore the nature of your prejudice without fear of reprisal." That seems to me one of the fundamentally important things about natural history writing: considering other ways of living—the culture, for example, of wolves—or considering the almost ungraspable life, the colonial life, of insects. In any consideration of some particular facet of the natural world, you are able to examine your own prejudices—to organize according to your own culture, to think that you are the grander, to think that you are the one in control—and no animal is going to turn around and strike you. The reaction is one of indifference. So I think now we are coming back to this position where we recognize that for so many thousands of years the natural world gave us our clothing, our food, our shelter. It was the source of humor for us. It was the ground against which we constructed our stories. And now, again, many tens of thousands of years later, the natural world is still there, still giving to us to help us in this difficult journey that we have chosen as human beings, to help us in this incredible intellectual risk that we have taken. The traditional idea that the animals are helpers is still relevant today in our highly sophisticated, academic, end-of-the-twentieth-century environment. And the notion that the natural world is a gift is, I think, something that floats in the best natural history writing.

LUEDERS: Gentlemen, may we invite others in the room into your dialogue? A question or two from the audience?

WILSON: We've already told you everything we know, but we can try. [laughter]

QUESTION: Dr. Wilson, I was just wondering if you can give two or three reasons for the hominid cranial explosion two million years ago?

WILSON: That's the grandmother of questions. You know, life was on the earth for over three and a half billion years before the first cultural species appeared, and, when that appeared, it literally almost exploded into existence. So why this one species achieved a cultural capacity is the central question of human evolution. *Newsweek* and *Time* and the rest of the media seem to be preoccupied with the length of the thigh bone and whether early people were gathering tubers or spearing antelopes. But the real question is, what happened up here in the brain? And what kind of genetic cum cultural process was and is going on?

I suspect that some sort of threshold was reached in which a reciprocity between cultural evolution and genetic evolution ignited so that culture broke free to act like rapid-fire mutations. New choices of behavior then put intense pressures on the underlying genes for capacitation of that potential, and that in turn caused the culture to leapfrog still farther ahead, and so on. The two then became a kind of oscillating motor that drove the cerebral cortex to a more than threefold increase in capacity. A large part of the change, when you think about it, was in straight long-term memory capacity. The mind consists substantially of processing of immense stores of memory, mostly symbolic but some episodic as well, through the channel of short-term memory whenever we do conscious thinking. We have this immense store up here, combined with changes in the parietal region of the brain, that has to do strictly with language processing. That in a nutshell is the key to human evolution, in my opinion. And so what sort of culture change was going on that was important? Well, it almost certainly was not just tool-making. That went rather slowly until quite recently in human history. But rather almost certainly language and, very likely, the formalization of human relationships through contractual arrangements, kin recognition, and the like. That's the best guess we have, but we don't have an answer

yet as to why the event occurred only once. And it won't happen
again, because our species took over the world and preempted the
origin of culture in other species.

QUESTION: A question for Mr. Lopez. You said earlier about how
you felt that your genre of writing, ahh . . . you felt that that gave
you the opportunity to greatly impact the world, and that was an
exciting thing for you, that you were making a difference by what
you were saying — the ability to express those things in nature writing. I'd like to know your self-perception. Do you feel — in the face
of what was brought up here about desertification, deforestation,
disappearance of species, etc., and those being the absolutely criti-
cal issues of our day — do you find yourself, in your own perceptions
of yourself and your writing — do you find yourself being — say, met-
aphorically — a stone thrown in a still and stagnant pond that's going
to affect all of the remnants thereof? Or do you find yourself a peb-
ble in a stream that rushes around you? Of course, you make the
stream go around you — but it rushes on down the stream. How do
you perceive yourself?

LOPEZ: I just write. [laughter, applause]

LUEDERS: And I encourage you to do the same. [more laughter]

LOPEZ: I don't mean to be disrespectful about the question, but I am
trying to be honest. I don't ever think about those things. The most
that I think about is how to understand something, how to show my
regard for the place where I am and for the people I travel with and
for the animals that I am around so that when I come back to my
home, to my own culture, I will be able to tell a story that is a good
story, that is fundamentally sound as well as I can make it — and ask
of the reader to grant me fallibility, the same that we all recognize
in each other. Whether the work has an effect or not is not what
drives me. My passion is language and landscape, and those two
are inseparable for me. That is where the focus of my life is. What
happens, or what I might feel as an individual man about the right-
ness of this or that or the other thing, is immaterial or is no more
important than what anyone else here thinks. After you write down
what you have to say, after you tell the story, then the story has an
effect of its own, and it's translated or it is shared because people

find it good enough to share. I don't think of myself as having any kind of effect, but I am often reminded that I share with other writers this very awkward personal situation. If your work is well known, a sort of spotlight comes on you and you are supposed to be, or you are made to be, more important than you are. And my sense of affection for other natural history writers — I dislike that term; it's such a confining term — is the sense of the enterprise that we have embarked on together. If the spotlight is on one or another of us at the time, well, that's how the world works. But each of us is making a contribution to something that all of us believe in, which is enlightenment, bringing light into this dark forest. And the sense that you might be having an effect — I don't really think about it. I think instead about this word — I think it's in *Arctic Dreams* — this Inuktitut word *isumatag*, which means the storyteller. *Isumatag* is the person who creates the atmosphere in which wisdom reveals itself. And so the burden is not on you as a writer to be wise. The burden on you as a writer is to be responsible.

I remember telling some students one time that the essence of nonfiction writing is to make a bow of respect toward the material, not to condescend — to make a proper inquiry, to have patience, to spend a long time, to allow yourself to be tutored as well as you can, not to project, to try to hear. And after that bow of respect toward the material, you turn and make a bow of respect toward the reader, which is to say that you owe the reader as a member of your community clarity and coherence, a certain elegance of language, as well as you can manage that. That's what you owe in your community. And then whether the story you have told is good or not, the people will decide that. Of course, you have to deal with the commercial apparatus of publishing and all of these things that we can be cynical about. But it seems to me essentially important to recognize that you are part of something. You are working with material that is much larger than the dimensions of your own scientific vision or your own artistic vision and you are a member of a community. And it is the community that must have an effect, if we are to do what we believe. We must establish some sense of reciprocity with the Earth, some sense of what is owed back and forth. We have abrogated those agreements through the industrial revolution and the agricultural revolution. We have abrogated those traditional treaties that existed between people and landscape. And we are trying to suture that wound now. And the way that we do it — the way that I do it — is depending on minds like yours to tell me as a writer, "Look at this. Pay attention to this connection. Are you aware of this? Do you know this?" This is the kind of heuristic guidance that comes to me as a writer. This and my own devotion and care about language, my own delight in seeing what happens to a human face that hears a story — putting those two things together, then setting the book out on its own and backing away, going back and doing your work.

Last summer a group of us — Gary Snyder, myself, Gary Nabhan, and some other people many of you know — were all together for a symposium in Alaska. And somebody made some remark that provoked me to say that we seemed to be losing a very important thread of what I would call the moral dimension of language in our discussions. In addition to its dimensions that are instructive or didactic or passing on information or entertaining, language has a moral dimension. I felt compelled to say something about that, and I did. Then afterward I was walking with one of the so-called students, and this person said to me, "You know, we depend on you people — you and Snyder and these other people — to write. To write. It's not necessary for you to stand publicly for something or to run for office or to do these other things. We depend on you for what you write." What he was telling me — what he was reiterating to me — was a belief that I had lost sight of in that moment, which is that we are a community. And if we don't have that sense of community, that sense of support, that we are a group of scientists, a group of writers, a group of teachers — if we don't have this, then what threatens us will destroy us. We have to have this kind of diversity in the shapes of our minds, and we have to create an atmosphere of dignity and mutual respect if we are ever going to do anything about whatever the hell it is out there that destroys animals, that destroys forests, that destroys human beings, that wipes out human cultures, that destroys initiative, and that tells people who are inarticulate or crippled that there is no place for them in the world. So I just write. [applause]

WILSON: A point of difference in style, as you've just seen illustrated perhaps, is the difference between a professor who is trying to write and a real writer. [laughter] I've struggled in all the writing I've done against the professional impulse to write pedagogically, in the style that seems to imply, "Pay attention because, yes, this is going to be on the final exam." [more laughter] I don't know if I will ever be able to write in quite the manner that you just described, Barry.

LOPEZ: But you do already.

WILSON: I appreciate very much those who can do it with that style and that intention in mind.

LUEDERS: Gentlemen, we are grateful. I think we are fortunate, Barry and Ed, to have you as members of our community. I mean that both in relation to your brief visit with us and in the larger sense that you are natural resources who are unnatural in your skills and in your generosity.

As for the method that we have just used here, I am reminded of a quotation from *Moby Dick* — that great work of natural history — by Herman Melville, who traveled the globe and came back to tell the tale as Ishmael, the wanderer. I quoted this to you earlier today, and I want to cement it in place for you because I think it is testimony to what has happened this evening. It is the first sentence of the chapter in *Moby Dick* called "The Honor and Glory of Whaling," which begins with the statement: "There are some enterprises in which a careful disorderliness is the true method." We're grateful, and thank you very much, for your careful disorderliness this evening. [applause]

Dialogue Two

LANDSCAPE, PEOPLE, AND PLACE

Robert Finch and
Terry Tempest Williams

February 8, 1988

ROBERT FINCH has been a staff member of the Bread Loaf Writers' Conference in Middlebury, Vermont. His books *Common Ground: A Naturalist's Cape Cod*, *The Primal Place*, and *Outlands: Journeys to the Outer Edges of Cape Cod,* personalize his sense of place. Mr. Finch wrote the foreword for the anniversary edition of Aldo Leopold's *Sand County Almanac*. He is editing *The Norton Book of Nature Writing* and working on a book about Newfoundland.

TERRY TEMPEST WILLIAMS is Naturalist-in-Residence at the Utah Museum of Natural History. Her book *Pieces of White Shell* received the 1984 Southwest Book Award for creative nonfiction. Smithsonian Magazine called it "a modern day myth of magic and wonder." She is also the author of two nature books for young people, *The Secret Language of Snow*, with Ted Major, and *Between Cattails*. Her most recent publications are *Earthly Messengers; Coyote's Canyon,* in collaboration with photographer John Telford; and *Refuge.*

LUEDERS: Welcome to the second in the series of conversations in our extended living room on "Writing Natural History." The two authors with us tonight are Terry Tempest Williams from our own Great Basin and Robert Finch from Cape Cod, Massachusetts. I have had the privilege and pleasure of sharing their home ground with each of them — with Terry, on many occasions in our own area, and with Bob Finch, walking his woods with him in Brewster, Massachusetts, last fall.

I think the best place to start our conversation takes off from the program title we gave to this pairing, "Landscape, People, and Place." These two authors' books are combinations of natural history, a sense of place, and humanity. Each has become identified with peculiar and particular landscapes. Mr. Finch comes from Cape Cod and has written three remarkable books on that area. And Terry Tempest Williams has written distinctively about the Great Basin and our western landscapes. I think we will move from east to west the way the country has and begin with Cape Cod. I'd like to ask each of you — Bob Finch, first — about your motivations, about your sense of working a place and your own vision of it into literature.

FINCH: Thank you, Ed. Having heard about last week's dialogue, I feel this chair is very large — but comfortable. What I am going to do is kind of an experiment. I want to read two statements, more or less in reply to Ed's question. There is a connection between them. I'm not sure what it is yet. Maybe we'll work it out through the evening.

"We are what we imagine ourselves to be. We are where we imagine ourselves to be. Yesterday morning, as our plane lifted off from Los Angeles International Airport, we swung out over the wide magnificent beaches of Malibu and Santa Monica, out over the blue waters of the Pacific, like some endless, glassy pool on whose surface patterns of sails and hulls were scattered like white flower petals. Further out, beyond the boats, the abrupt flattened islands of the offshore hung, floated, cradled in a purple haze. Then the plane banked steeply to the left and swung inland over the intricate circuitry and the vast human design of the Los Angeles megalopolis. Surely, I thought, this is one of the most magnificent landscapes in the world, however soiled or defiled it has become. I waited expectantly for some gesture of recognition, some acknowledgement of its wonder and of the wonder of our ability to soar and move above it in a breadth and pace of motion commensurate with that of the scene itself. The pilot's perfunctory voice squeaked out, 'On your right side, just below, is Dodger Stadium.' A long pause, a steady thrum of turbines, then: 'On the left is Pasadena, home of the Rose Bowl.' Then at last, coming up out of the valley, we moved directly over the great rumpled green velvet flanks of the San Bernardino Mountains, their highest crests lapped, as with ermine, in spotted snow. I looked down on majesty — serene, indifferent to its still puny human denigrations, knowing how many changes of clothes it has had and will have over the ages. Over the address system, the captain informed us, 'To the north, just left of the wing, you can see Edwards Air Force Base, site of many of the space shuttle recoveries.' We mark the landscape to our dimensions with games and technological toys while the land waits for its proper cartographers.

"Nature writers attempt to create enduring myths of our relationship to the land and other creatures. They story the landscape, often using themselves as a kind of Everyman or Everywoman figure, trying to frame representative responses, gestures, attitudes, utterances, contacts with the earth that will illuminate that relationship. Their words and books not only help us to see and understand; in a real sense, they create what we see and shape our understanding. Just as people who live for a long time in one place tend to see and recognize places in terms of events that occurred or were said to occur there, so the consciousness of our poets and writers is associated with our various landscapes. We see not just seashores, ponds, rivers, mountains, marshes, forests, and plains. But we see Thoreau's reflective Walden, John Muir's Range of Light, Faulkner's Big Woods, Henry Beston's Great Beach of Cape Cod, Loren Eiseley's Night Country of the Plains, Robinson Jeffers's Big Sur, Aldo Leopold's Round River, Mary Austin's Land of Little Rain, Annie Dillard's tree with lights at Tinker Creek, Barry Lopez's arctic dreamscape, and on and on. These are not just places, but states of mind, rituals and explorations of the psyche, attempts to redefine who we are and where we are. This is ultimately as important as any body of purely ecological information or knowledge, for ultimately we can only care for and connect with that which we have come to love. I think that only by storying the earth do we come to love it, does it become the place where imagination chooses to reside. By storying the place where we live, it gives us back a sense of who and where we are. Through stories, we literally identify with the land. We love what we come to call home. Nature writers teach us to recognize home."

WILLIAMS: I think all writers must confront their own biases so that they might see their world more clearly and ultimately be freed by those biases. And so I am here to tell you that I write through my biases of gender, geography, and culture, that I am a woman whose ideas have been shaped by the Colorado Plateau and the Great Basin, that these ideas are then sorted out through the prism of my culture—and my culture is Mormon. Those tenets of family and community that I see at the heart of that culture are then articulated through story.

I will tell you that I am a naturalist first and a writer second, that the landscape came before the words. I have an image at a very early age—as an infant, actually—of being on a blanket with my mother on one corner, my grandmother on the other corner, and my aunt on the other. The image that I remember is having to cross the grass to get to my mother or grandmother or aunt. I remember the feeling of the grass in the palms of my hands—a sensation that was new to me, that was curious, that was at times frightening. And I remember pulling back, seeking the safety of that blanket. But then I remember the absolute hunger of going out. New territory: a place to discover, to learn from and, in time, to serve. A recognition of the earth came before the words.

It seems that our family has always been obsessed with this business of geography. When I talk about writing natural history, I must begin where I have always begun, and that is with my family. Of being told stories around the table about how my grandmother, Lettie Romney, left Chihuahua, Mexico, to come to the so-called "promised land"—that at a moment's notice they were told to get on their horses, and my great-grandmother, Vilate Lee Romney, put my grandmother on a bundle around her back and left the cake cooking in the oven. I remember being told, on another side of the family, of my great-great-grandfather, who was asked by Brigham Young to serve a mission in St. George, Utah, which he dutifully did. It was usually a two- to three-year period. Four years, five years, six years, seven years later he was still serving in St. George. Finally his wife pleaded with him, "Please, if you just ask Brother Brigham, I feel certain he would return you home to us." His reply was simple. "We must be patient. I have been called to serve the Lord in Dixie." Then one day he finally got enough courage, got on his horse, and traveled for days up to Salt Lake City and knocked on the door of the Beehive House. He said, "Brother Brigham, I'm Brother Romney. I've been serving eight years in St. George." Brigham Young put his hand firmly on the missionary's shoulder and said, "I'm so glad you came back, Brother Romney, we had forgotten where we sent you." [laughter]

That kind of devotion to people and place is what was discussed around our dinner table. Stories of Eureka, Utah, then a booming mining town where my grandmother, Kathryn Blackett, and my great-aunt, Marion, were held ransom, and of how my great-grandfather, Lawrence Blackett, left the money in a bag under the designated rock with a note saying, "My family is worth far more than any amount of money." My grandmother and aunt were released. And I remember my other grandmother talking about picking beets in Cornish, Utah. We were raised on the value of family. Cornish, Eureka, St. George — these are not obscure towns in my family. They have taken on mythic proportions. They teach us where we come from and what we are a part of. To me, Utah was the promised land and always has been. It is refuge, and it has been handed down to the children, generation after generation. Brigham Young said, "This is the place," and there are those of us who still believe that.

I do not mean to sound provincial. I merely want to provide insight into my own sense of place. And I think if each of you were to sit in this chair, you would have your own story about your own place to tell. I suspect that you find in your way the same passion that I do in the natural world.

My ties to Utah do not end here. My family for four generations has been laying pipe in the Utah substrate. So we are a family of pipeline contractors. Although I have never dug the ditches, I have cared for the men — my brothers, my father, my uncles, my grandfather, and my great-grandfather — who have. Digging in the earth, making bids as to whether the ground beneath our feet was granite or sand or that fresh, fertile till. Our lives depended on it. My father taught us at an early age that nothing is as it appears, that you must dig deep, make test holes, and find out for yourself. I remember as a small child standing with him as he would calculate and read the landscape and talk to us about what we saw and what was really there. He taught us that a great error enters when we assume that there are no other levels than the one we see. And then at 6:15 p.m., around the dinner table, conversations stopped. We listened to the weather. It meant whether or not the company would work the next day.

There was a fierce awareness of the forces outside of ourselves — call it ditchdigging humility. We learned that this is tough country, that you work hard, that you dig deep, that you lay the pipe and you cover it up and no one really ever sees what you do. But you do it well, because people's homes, their heat and their electricity, depend on that work. This kind of childhood, this kind of background has influenced me deeply, and I value this sense of belonging . . . [her voice breaks; there is an emotion-filled pause]

FINCH: [wanting to help] You know . . . may I break in?

WILLIAMS: I can finish. [she resumes] . . . this sense of belonging to a people and a place with a tradition.

Words have now become the medium through which my questions of gender, geography, and culture can be explored. The natural world has become a practice, a teaching, the place where I can make peace with my own contradictory nature, the place where we all can make peace with our own contradictory natures. I write about what I know, and I am inspired by what I don't know — which is enormous. I believe in the longing for unity, that we may in fact be asking for a new way to think about science but in reality are asking for a new way to think about ourselves, that this yearning to heal the fragmentation and divisions that separate us from nature, that separate us from ourselves, that separate us from God or the mysteries, that this longing for unity has everything to do with

family, with community and the landscape we are a part of. As Ed
Lueders says, "Thus we write natural history." We must begin to
act on our own understandings.

LUEDERS: I'm going to suggest a common note that I heard in those
two statements, and that's the element of story—history itself, natural or otherwise, as story. And I'm going to wonder out loud about
the relationship of story or narrative to its basis in fact and observation, which is essential to natural history from the angle of the
naturalist as well as the writer. There is some sort of matrix here
that I experience in reading your work, Bob, and in yours, too,
Terry, where storytelling—narrative—is an essential part of the
writer's way of dealing with natural history. And I wonder if this is
something you might elaborate on from your own points of view.

FINCH: Okay. Indirectly, if I might. That was a very brave statement you made, Terry, and I feel I should catch up in some way.
    I live in a place—Cape Cod—that is probably one of the old-
est settled areas on the continent, one of the most storied parts of
the country in a literal sense, and a place that has a kind of symbolic meaning or some imaginative resonance in the minds of a lot
of people, which makes them get in their cars and drive and clog
our streets every summer. And it has to do with something more
than Patti Page's song about old Cape Cod. There is a special character to Cape Cod, certainly, and I feel fortunate living there. But I
think part of what attracted me to it was its storied quality, the local
history, which went deep and was colorful, the fact that it had a
literary tradition. Unlike Terry, I began as a writer first and then
kind of wormed my way into natural history by hanging around
naturalists and parasitizing them. So I came to natural history writing, or nature writing, through a love of literature, of story. I began
in a fairly conventional way writing stories.
    When I came to the Cape—for I grew up in a city, or, rather,
several cities—I felt a strong attraction to the area, which I didn't
understand. I also felt as though it were the place where I should
have been born, as though it were the place where I would have had
that kind of rootedness that you talk about, Terry. And I think a lot
of what I do is an attempt to imagine for myself that rootedness in
the place where I have chosen to live. A lot of people do that,
though not professionally. A lot of people come to Cape Cod not

just because it's a pleasant place to live but because of its sense of history, which is ultimately a sense of story, and they can borrow a sense of history from the land. We're nearly all what they call "wash-ashores" on Cape Cod. And we all become instant natives, and outdo the real natives, and adopt all the trappings. It is a way of seeking identity for our age, which has trouble sensing identity — at least in the part of the country where I live, where most people can't go back to the site of their childhood because it's a shopping mall or it's a parking lot or whatever. We all do that to some degree.

I think a lot of what I do is making up stories about the place I live and how I live there — but making up by interacting with it. I don't mean I sit in my room and make up stories. You read those kinds; you know what they are. And I've wondered from time to time if that's valid — you know, the individual writer making up stories and attempting to live them. It's a strange feeling sometimes now that I'm a published writer and I take a writer's liberty occasionally of giving names to things that don't have names. There's an area of our town that I invented the word "punkhorn" for, and now a lot of people go around talking about "the Punkhorn." There is even a Punkhorn Realty Corporation. [laughter]

WILLIAMS: So you're creating your own mythology.

FINCH: Well, yes. I mean it's literally true: stories create meaning. They create the way you see the land. That's a very simple example. But all of a sudden I realize that I'm part of the process, and it's a great responsibility. What kind of stories am I creating, anyway? They'd better be good ones. I hope they are. But it's nice, too. You know, I envy you, Terry, a lot of what you have — that you were born in the place that you choose to write about and have all that history behind you. In addition, you have the accessibility or availability to a living oral culture with the Navajo, as you've demonstrated in *Pieces of White Shell*. In other words, by reading your book, I sensed that they were at least close enough to directly influence the way you thought about yourself and your own history.

WILLIAMS: Back up, just a minute, you say you envy what I have, yet your mother and father live in your same town.

FINCH: Yes, but it was just the opposite. They followed me there.

WILLIAMS: But that's wonderful. [laughter]

FINCH: It can be. Where I live, that pattern is very common. And sometimes it works out, and sometimes it doesn't. In our case, it worked out. Family is implicit in a lot of my writings, but I don't write directly about it. Family and community are there, yes, but I hope it's implicit. You know, one of the standard criticisms that nature writers get is that we're misanthropes, we're antisocial. Because you love whales, you can't like people. Or because you don't mention people enough. I once submitted a proposal for a book to a publisher who shall remain unnamed, and the response was, "Well, yes, we like the proposal, but could you put a little more people in it."

WILLIAMS: I believe within this notion of people and place, story is the correspondence between the two. It informs our lives, it keeps things known. It's the umbilical cord between the past, present, and future. Story identifies the relationships, and I think that's what is essential in the heart of good storytelling—and also a good nature walk—to be able to see those inherent relationships. The classic case: I remember on the reservation it had just rained and we had gone out onto the slickrock and there were some yucca. You know yucca?

FINCH: I know yucca. It grows on Cape Cod, too. [laughter]

WILLIAMS: Y-u-c-c-a. [more laughter] Anyway, the children said, "tsa-aszi," which means yucca in Navajo, and I remember one of the Navajo children asking, "What story does this tell?" And that changed my life, because I realized it's not only in terms of human interaction that we find story informs and instructs, but also in the natural world. Everything is subject to story. Everything is related. Well, then the children went on. I took them very seriously. Being the good naturalist that I thought I was, I began to tell them that this is *Yucca augustissima*, that there is this moth that pollinates it and sticks its ovipositor in the plant's ovary and lays its eggs . . . And they got completely bored and ran over to another yucca plant, turned it upside down, got out a pocket knife, cut open one of the roots, and sliced it in four. Then they ran over to a pothole in the slickrock. Brian dunked his head in the pothole, as Loren began lathering up the yucca, creating suds, and started washing his hair. I'm still back there with practically no audience, you know, trying to tell them "what story this tells." Finally, the girls left. They came back with a clutch of mountain grass, and as Brian was drying his hair, they began to comb it. And then I remember saying, "That's wonderful. What would happen if I washed my hair with yucca?" And they said, "Sorry, it would give you warts." [laughter] But it impressed on me the idea that a story defines a group. And a story can be shared to elucidate the nature of that group. And the story grows. A story is never finished. A story has a life of its own, and it's creating that perpetually new mythology, so to speak, that grows out of the earth. I wonder what stories we tell that evoke a sense of place?

FINCH: You know, coming from a place where the indigenous people were never available, we have no oral native tradition. It's one of the ironies of anthropology on this continent that we know much less about the eastern tribes than we know about the western tribes, because in the east they disappeared and dissipated, for the most part, so fast. So that's not available at all to inform and draw from. Even with the local culture which I have tried to incorporate into a lot of my writing, I realize what I was doing was running around trying to snatch up the last things before they disappeared.

I mean, to talk about a living local culture in a place like Cape Cod doesn't make sense in the way that I would have liked it to have made sense. I would have liked to have participated in the long-rooted continuum of living with the land. It was a very rich culture and had to do with all the things that you're talking about — knowing what it took to make a living on the land. There remains a viable fishing culture, and that's probably the closest that there is to it. And there are the crafts, the forms that have become part of our lives: the Cape Cod house, which is the standard frame dwelling and was very well adapted to that particular area; the whole art of bird carving, which began with observation from people who had pragmatic interests in knowing how to make decoys; that kind of thing — tools adapted to the land. Well, that's part of the richness of living in a place like the Cape, and that's all available to some degree. But still there's something missing, and I think that that's a lot of the impetus for what I do. We not only need to have a tradition or history of stories, we have to be part of something that's ongoing — which is what you were talking about, Terry, to some degree. And that's why I made that kind of opening statement, saying that I see a lot of the function of nature writers as an attempt to begin to create new myths.

WILLIAMS: Do you take the land literally?

FINCH: Do I take it literally?

WILLIAMS: Yes. I mean when you're out in it. I guess what I'm wondering about is this business of landscape as metaphor.

FINCH: Oh, I see. Well, not in the sense of using the landscape as symbol. At least that's fairly minor. I realized early on that there was something about the basic shape of my imagination that was answered by the Cape's landscape in some way. I mean it was what was out there. It wasn't that I was raiding the landscape for nice metaphors. If anything, the land was raiding me, taking me literally. And so the writing is a kind of an exploration of what that correspondence is, and I have given it various answers over the years.

Cape Cod has what I call an extraordinary human scale. The land itself is very gentle, very small. The features of the landscape tend to be diminutive. Distances are short. You can't go very far without hitting water. And it's something vulnerable. It's all glacial till, sand dune — things which are very easily altered. The soil blew away three hundred years ago when they first cut down the trees, and it's never come back. And the forests are very stunted everywhere. The overriding presence of the ocean defines the character of that land, and the ocean is change. That's not a metaphor; that's a reality. The ocean is mutable. It changes things. *It* changes. And on Cape Cod we see our geography, our topography, changed over our lifetime. It seems to have a scale that answers to the human scale of motion. So that's one of the correspondences I see.

WILLIAMS: I loved — I think it was in *The Primal Place* — when you talked about . . . Was it Conrad Aiken who said he's never seen a dead squirrel in his woods?

FINCH: Lewis Thomas.

WILLIAMS: Lewis Thomas. And you were saying how when you see that wrack line you are constantly seeing the evidence of life and death.

FINCH: Yes. It's life in the open on the shore. But I think that's true out here, too. If you live in a suburban woodland, then you are not going to see many dead things. But certainly the ocean almost aggressively reminds you of the presence of death as part of the whole cycle. Thoreau, when he visited it, was really appalled — one of the few times, you know, something cracked that hard shell — when he was on the beach and he referred to the ocean as "a vast morgue." Nature was "inhumanly sincere," he said. There's always that contrast where I live between the ocean on one side and the fragile stability of the land on the other. When I say the ocean and I say change, I say chaos, I say violence — that, to me, is not metaphor. Its reality is the source from which we get notions like change.

So, as a writer — I'm going to shift gear a little bit here — as a writer, I see the exploration of nature as a way of getting at the roots of a great deal of human meaning — that it is *literally* our source of meaning. It has to be. It is, superficially, just on the level of language. Language comes from nature. Etymologically, language goes back to natural facts, appearances, whatever. We've lost the sense of that, but it's true. But, more than that, we find our values there. And storytelling is a way of doing that. I hadn't thought a lot about that before coming out here, but storytelling is something that our culture tends to see by and large as entertainment. So you tell me a story before I go to bed —

LUEDERS: Or passively watch half-hour segments on TV.

FINCH: Right. Instead of, as you're presenting it, Terry, as a basic way of understanding and participating in the creation.

WILLIAMS: I think we're in a curious time. We know so much and it's so easy to become so analytical and everything is explained and we shy away from mystery or from ambiguity. Yet that which is uniquely human and that which is so beautiful about our species is the ability to make meaning, to symbolize. And I think, by taking everything literally in the stories we tell, that we're really denying our own depths.

FINCH: One of the encouraging things I find—and you had a perfect example of this in last week's dialogue—is the participation in this process of storytelling, this thinking by metaphor, of scientists—people like E. O. Wilson who are respected scientists in their own field and also have this literary side and this desire to explore their subject in a personal way and, in doing so, tell wonderful stories. I find that very encouraging because in the tradition of naturalists there originally was not that split that we see today between the humanities and the sciences. A naturalist in the eighteenth or the early nineteenth century was expected to be well-educated in the humanities and also to have a sense of style. He was not afraid to use his human responses in describing what he was studying. Some of the passages I use to illustrate what nature writing can do I take from Charles Darwin. Darwin was a wonderful writer and risked his own sense of the enormity of the subject he was dealing with, the sense of wonder at what he was looking at. And that's so often missing in people who know the most about the subject, because they withhold themselves from that process.

WILLIAMS: You know, if you are talking about metaphor and Earth, the real metaphor of our time, it strikes me, is the Earth-rise, the way that in our lifetime we see the Earth not apart from the Heaven, not Heaven being there and Earth here. But, rather, Earth is *in* the heavens, and we literally find ourselves in a free fall. There are no more horizons, just infinite space. And I was thinking that there is this new story to be told. If in fact we are in free fall, we can relax, because we also know there is no ground—so that there's no need for a parachute unless we want to slow down. Do you know what I mean?

LUEDERS: Terry, I'd like to bring you down to earth. [laughter] Using the word "earth" is my cue, because I find that a whole view of the Earth . . .

WILLIAMS: I was serious. I was really serious.

LUEDERS: . . . involves a portrait much like the Cape Cod landscape. The emphasis falls upon the ocean and upon that irregular
configuration of land that is an interruption of the ocean, which is
dominant on our planet. But, in the Great Basin area that you work
in as a naturalist and as a writer and as a storyteller, the reverse is
true. We have here earth as a dominant reality and water as the
transient — as the element that comes and goes and empties into the
Great Basin in the form of what remains of Lake Bonneville, that is,
the Great Salt Lake, which goes up and down in comparatively
small ways.

WILLIAMS: Nowadays, we just pump it away. [laughter]

LUEDERS: I'd like to hear your evocation of the area that you work in
as a writer, because it seems to me that it has such an additional
thing to say about the United States as nature writers' fare and perhaps complementary to what Bob has given us. How do you feel
about the land you write about?

WILLIAMS: It's tough, you know. It's tough to talk about because it's
like my skin. Very close. It's a lean landscape perfect for draping
ideas over. Nothing is as it appears. Think about the Great Salt
Lake. For most of us along the Wasatch Front, it's largely a back-
drop for our sunsets. Or maybe we went there ritualistically as a
child. The adults sacrificed themselves and their station wagons to
take you out and let you run in the lake, which you did enthusias-
tically until you got up to your knees where all the scrapes and
scratches on your legs were and the salt burned — and you ran out
and you went home and you never thought about it again. It's been
a pleasure for me to return to the lake, seeing it now as self-
proclaimed wilderness. We may think we can spend $60 million
and pump the lake into the west desert, and we might hope it will
be an international tourist attraction when that no longer is necessary. But the fact remains the lake will always be exactly who it is,
that there is that trickster quality about it. The Great Basin — the
mirages that are there — it's a dreamscape. And in a lot of ways I
think it is a sophisticated landscape because it takes a long, long
time to see it. It takes a long, long time to travel through it. It asks
us to redefine what is beautiful.

LUEDERS: This is a matter of space, but it is also a matter of time, then. You know, as a native midwesterner, I really ought to be between the two of you here, geographically speaking. Being raised in Chicago, I learned to think east to Lake Michigan, northward into the north woods and lakes of Wisconsin, south below Indianapolis into the rolling possibilities of the Ohio River Valley, and west into Iowa and the cornfields. But everything farther west was mirage, until I came here and discovered that the firm earth was primary once you got beyond Denver—not simply to fructify and to turn the seasons over and grow things but, beyond that, to have time sequences built in that are geological, and that match the sense of open space. And I find, when I visited your woods, for instance, Bob, knowing that the ocean was hard by, that that combination was such a different experience even though it's part of the same country.

FINCH: You know, that's the fallacy a lot of people have. We feel that we have removed ourselves from local environment. I mean, we recognize, if we are at all enlightened, that we are dependent upon basic processes. We have to worry about water quality and such things. But we don't feel that we're really affected by local environment. We can get in our houses, get in our cars. We can move, if we don't like where we are. But I find that—and this is one of the things that make me feel that I work in a real tradition, because the basic facts remain the same—we're still human beings, finite organisms with certain shapes, specific senses. And whether we admit it or not to ourselves, we're affected in very subtle but complex ways by where we live.

One example is the woods you mentioned, which are recent on Cape Cod. A hundred years ago there weren't any. Three hundred years before that it was all—or nearly all—forests. It comes and goes. Everything is recent on the Cape. You talked about geological time. On Cape Cod what you see is no more than fifteen thousand years old, made by the last glacier. And I've thought to myself sometimes: I live in a land that, at most, is going to be around for another six thousand years. Given the present rate of sea level rise, maybe less, the way things are going. What does it mean to live in a place that has almost a human, finite breadth of existence compared to the kind of place that you're in here? Well, if you look at all and feel at all, it does give you a sense of change. And if you don't look, you're in deep trouble—in lots of ways.

Here again, we're a very seasonal land. That's something, I think, that is very characteristic about Cape Cod. Most people know it only from the summer. It's a summer place in the mind. I've known many people who think of themselves as good conservationists, members of the Audubon Society or the Sierra Club who give to the funds to protect tern colonies or whatever. They've come to the Cape for summers on end, and finally they decide that they'd like to live there. And the best place to live, of course, is right on the water, next to that nice, gentle, broad beach. Although the waterfront property has gotten pretty expensive, they think that it's worth it. So they buy it, and they move. And September comes— September's the loveliest month that we have on the Cape. October isn't bad either. In November the first northeasters start, and all of a sudden the beach seems to be getting narrower and a little steeper, and the ocean doesn't look like what it looked like in the summer. One day they wake up and they find waves lapping at the door. Then they run to the local contractor and say, "What do we do about this? Can you put some stones on the beach?" And he says, "Well, you have to go to the Conservation Commission to do that." So they go to the Conservation Commission, and they fill out all the intricate forms, and we inform them that we couldn't let them do it even if we wanted to. There's a state law against those kinds of structures on the beach because they have complex environmental effects, et cetera, et cetera. All of a sudden they become the strongest property rights advocates in the world. Because they see, in fact, that the place where they live has a will of its own, and it isn't always the will that they want it to have.

WILLIAMS: You know, Bob—forgive me for interrupting, but this business of the politics of place concerns me. You live in a place that is highly valued and has an incredibly rich tradition of romance and literature and prestige. In the Great Basin and in the Colorado Plateau, we don't live in what is considered a desirable place. The place that we live in is largely seen as country for a nuclear waste repository or the MX racetrack or the Nevada Test Site or land suitable for holding nerve gas. And—forgive me for saying this— but when you arrived and said, "Well, you know Salt Lake is in the middle of nowhere," and with a twinkle in your eye added "everywhere" . . . Well, I think there is that notion that space in the west means empty space, wasted space. I'm concerned about this.

FINCH: You mean how people here view what they have?

WILLIAMS: No, not how we view it — how an eastern power base views the land we live in. There's a story concerning Canyonlands National Park. Lavender Canyon, adjacent to the park, was being considered for a nuclear waste repository site. A friend of ours was asked to pick up a woman who was drawing up the maps and the grids for the Department of Energy. He picked her up at the Moab airport. She said, "Will you take me to the hotel?" He said, "No. I'm taking you to see something." He then took her out to a particular vantage point in Canyonlands, and he said nothing. She got out her map, and, pointing, she said, "Lavender Canyon?" And he said, "Lavender Canyon." And she said, "My God! I had no idea." An empty spot on a map in the west means wild country. In the east it simply means void of population.

FINCH: Well, I don't think that's peculiar to the west. Although I think what you said has a rough truth to it.

WILLIAMS: It's our land, you know, and the people who are making the decisions don't have a sense of that kind of space. We're dispensable. We're viewed by the Department of Defense as "an expendable segment of this nation's population" as seen in the aboveground nuclear testing in Nevada from 1953 to 1962.

FINCH: Well, yes. But again from my perspective . . .

WILLIAMS: We're Dixie cups.

FINCH: Well, listen, while Ed gets us another drink , I have a joke I want to tell.

WILLIAMS: This isn't a joke.

FINCH: I know it's no joke. But I have a joke that I'm not sure I'm going to get to work in any other way. It's the only good Cape Cod story that I have. And there's a serious point to it. One of the things I do like about folklore — I use that word now instead of storytelling or myth for stories that people still tell where we live — is that the best stories have a truth to them, a literal truth that people often miss. The example I was going to tell you was the old story on Cape Cod about the tourist who came down to the Cape and drove to Eastham to the site of Doane Rock. Doane Rock is a large glacial erratic—a large boulder—probably the biggest one on Cape Cod. When he drove up he saw the rock and there was an old Cape Codder sitting there on the fence. The tourist looked at the rock and said, "Big rock." And the Cape Codder said, "Ayuh." He said, "How did that rock get here?" And the Cape Codder said, "Glaciah brought it." The tourist said, "Oh, the glacier brought it, huh? That's interesting. Well, where's the glacier now?" "Went back for more rocks." [laughter] Thank you.

WILLIAMS: So I don't get it. [more laughter]

FINCH: Don't worry. I'm going to answer your question. I am.

WILLIAMS: And I'm not blaming you. The fact that you're from the east, you know—I still think you're a good person.

FINCH: Thanks. I expect to be treated with a certain tolerance as a guest here. [laughter]

WILLIAMS: [pouring glass of water] This is a gesture.

LUEDERS: Water is scarce in our parts. [more laughter]

FINCH: I appreciate it.

WILLIAMS: And it could be radioactive. [more laughter]

FINCH: Suddenly it's show time. All right. Yes, what you say is true about the eastern perspective on the west. Also—and I think this is significant—for most people in the east, the west is also the repository of wilderness. Okay? Wilderness has a certain value in people's minds, even if they have never seen it or have no desire to go there. And there are a lot of people who support the Wilderness Society and everything else out there. Actually, there is a wilderness area on Cape Cod. It's an officially designated National Wilderness Area, Monomoy Island Wilderness Area. But, for the most part, we think of wilderness as existing in the west. Save the wild lands of the west. So I think that is also part of the eastern perspective. Another thing: I think the emphasis in the environmental movement in the west is on wilderness. You know, let's keep wilderness wild; let's keep our wild lands purely wild. But in the east, that's not possible, really, so we don't try. I think the focus is a little different in the way we view nature, what we expect out of it. Having thought now a bit about the kind of writing I do, I find myself in a tradition that is very much eastern, that has a different focus. You pointed out one aspect of it to me in the comment you made about people like John Burroughs as opposed to John Muir, who went dancing over the mountain tops and exclaiming about God for forty years. John Burroughs would look at little birds, at little details.

WILLIAMS: You don't like John Muir?

FINCH: Hmmm?

WILLIAMS: I'm just kidding.

FINCH: No. I like John Muir. Johnny One Note.

WILLIAMS: But for Burroughs the focus was down, because of all the detail.

FINCH: For Burroughs and most eastern writers the focus was down and on small details, and then letting the detail expand into larger things. But there was also the presence of the human everywhere, and that's certainly a concept that I've mined in my writing. Once again, it's a truth. It's not just a metaphor. It's a real truth that our landscapes — certainly on Cape Cod, but most landscapes in New England — are different from what they were when the first settlers landed. And what you have now is often a very natural-looking landscape that is actually a resultant of human activity and natural processes — past human activities that have helped make it a natural-looking area. It's an interesting exercise to read a landscape historically from its environmental character and deduce all sorts of things about it.

But it also makes you raise larger questions that ask you to examine your own values, such as: What is a natural landscape? Why do we value a natural landscape as opposed to an artificial landscape? And is that a good thing? My personal perspective is that the most interesting landscapes are those in which there is some human presence, or at least not a place where human presence is artificially removed and has been replaced. When I go into a regulated wilderness, an officially designated wilderness, I always feel sad. I mean, I can enjoy it, but it tells me something about where we are and what we have to do. And, to me, that's a dead end. As much as I know that I would probably not be living on Cape Cod if it weren't for the Cape Cod National Seashore — because it stepped in in the nick of time to preserve the essence of a great deal of the place where I live — ultimately that approach to saving land I find a dead end.

WILLIAMS: Isn't it interesting because I find just the opposite. You know, we have the Lone Peak Wilderness area right here — twenty minutes away, literally — and I find that, when I am in the White Pine area, the minute I cross that line where it says "Lone Peak Wilderness" I feel as though I am stepping into sacred ground, that this is an area of sacred land that my culture has deemed important enough to leave alone. Let it be for its own sake. It has a life. It's an organism unto itself. I know I am safe there.

FINCH: Safe from what?

WILLIAMS: From encroachment. From public harassment. From the pressures of urban life that would deprive us of an authenticity of spirit.

FINCH: But then it's an escape. It's a refuge. It's not a place where you live. And I think what we have to do is to find a way to like the place where we live.

WILLIAMS: It's where my heart lives. Yes, it's where I go for refuge. But it's where I can see the pattern that connects, where I can go without the worry of a KOA campground or a Winnebago or a bastion of condominiums. I can be alone to contemplate, to remember where the source of my power lies — in the earth. I am renewed. Brought back to center.

FINCH: Okay, yeah.

WILLIAMS: It's the business of public land.

FINCH: But, but, but . . . Let me play devil's advocate a minute. Aren't you sort of being an aesthetic elitist? I mean you simply don't want to see the signs of civilization that you depend on. I don't mean just KOA campgrounds, but you want something different from where it is you have to live.

WILLIAMS: See, I don't think it is elitist. I think what's elitist is private land. Wilderness is public land in the most profound sense. It's there for everyone.

FINCH: Yes, but — well, it depends. Sometimes they establish quotas. A wilderness is a place with regulations.

WILLIAMS: And I think that's okay, too.

FINCH: But I find a contradiction between a wilderness that's regulated and the idea of wilderness.

LUEDERS: I'm going to interrupt with something that occurs to me in this conversation from the fact that both of you are affiliated with museums. And there is something in the wilderness area which is similar to the museum. Each of them holds in some relation to nature and natural fact things as they are, working as they work, within the larger sense of the Earth sphere we live in rather than in the small sphere of our own private lives. I wonder if there is anything worth exploring in this fact. The Utah Museum of Natural History is one of the sponsors of this program, and Terry is Naturalist-in-Residence for this museum. Your affiliation, as I understand it, Bob, is with the Cape Cod Museum as Director of Publications.

FINCH: It was.

LUEDERS: These are two different relationships, and it signals the fact that one of you is a writer who has the interests of a naturalist, the other a naturalist who has the skills and the vision of the writer. But I wonder if that museum association and point of view is pertinent to your work as well as to the questions of wilderness and the society which somehow wants to hold on to natural lands.

WILLIAMS: I wonder if you can say that wilderness is an institution. You know that a museum is an institution. It catalogs what we value. And, in terms of natural history, it preserves that which is natural — which is a dichotomy in a way, because the birds there are dead, yet we have their skins. But wilderness as an institution? I'm not sure. I really am not sure. When I'm in wilderness, I don't feel it's an institution. There is no ceiling or limitations. No human expectations that dictate its direction. When I'm in wilderness, I don't feel that it's contrived. It's what it is. And it's okay if we escape. I mean, yes, I am myself a dichotomy. I live in the city, and I go to the land to be refreshed. I think people have always done that on some level or another, in terms of that aesthetic need to be fed, to be still, to be calm, to be nourished — that whole idea of Mother Earth, if you want to get cosmic, Ed.

LUEDERS: When you write as a naturalist — when we write natural history — I wonder if there isn't some sort of conjunction of these two going on. When you write natural history, Terry — when you write natural history from your point of view and in your landscape — isn't there some configuration there that brings together that impulse of the museum, which is the society, the civilization, the culture . . .

WILLIAMS: An artifact.

LUEDERS: . . . together with the natural world, which you observe and bring into some sort of confluence?

WILLIAMS: Well, I think it has to do with the process, don't you, Bob? We were talking about that when we went out to Great Salt Lake yesterday. You go out and you experience it and you're part of the land, and then you come back in, you think about it, you intellectualize it, and you say, "All right. What did I just experience?" And then you go into all of the books about Lake Bonneville and Stansbury's report, and you sift through it and make some sort of sense of it all. It is a weaving. Again, I think that's part of being human, finding the meaning in our lives.

FINCH: There seems to be a natural pattern for a lot of nature writing. I know it is true in mine. Thoreau was probably the first one to really establish it. In a way *Walden* is atypical, though, because I think that the natural pattern for the nature essay is what he called "the excursion"—the venture out into something unknown or not familiar, something that he wanted to explore, and then coming back and shaping that experience into something. And I think it's a very natural form. That form is, if you will excuse the word, a metaphor for a more basic process, which is always an attempt of the mind to confront this wilderness that we call existence and to somehow shape meaning out of it. Maybe we ought to put that question of wilderness to rest at this point. But I wrote two essays in my first book that have "wilderness" in the title, "Wilderness Experience" and "Wilderness at the Run"—it's a little herring run in our town. I was trying to get across my experience that wilderness is where you find it and that it can happen, and usually does happen, in places that are not officially designated as wilderness areas.

WILLIAMS: Then maybe what we're really talking about is that sense of wildness.

FINCH: Wildness. Yes.

WILLIAMS: Remember what Thoreau said. He didn't say, in *wilderness* is the preservation of the world. It was, "In wildness is the preservation of the world."

FINCH: Yes. Yes. You're quite right.

LUEDERS: We have reached some sort of closure, or at least a significant pause. And we do want to invite the audience almost literally into our living room by way of their questions. Is there anything else that you would like to bring up from your points of view as writers of natural history before we make that turn in the program?

FINCH: I'm glad you asked. There is one thing Terry and I have discussed that I think impinges on this whole idea of landscape, but you don't get around to it naturally. Maybe that's symptomatic. You know, one charge that has been leveled at nature writers is that what they do is escapist literature, that there are really serious problems that need to be confronted in our time and just going out into the woods or the mountains or the plains or wherever and celebrating what you see there is really, in context, a trivial exercise.

This question was put to me very forcefully in an essay entitled "Self/Landscape/Grid" by a wonderful writer who recently died, Terrence Des Pres, who wrote about the threat of nuclear war, which is an omnipresent fact in our society, and how that impinges on the way we look at nature. The way he put it was that every landscape is part of a global nuclear grid; and with the recognition of that fact, how can one go out and simply explore one's personal responses? Is that not irresponsible? Is that not really trivializing what literature should be about, which is confronting the great issues of whatever time you live in? I loaned the essay to Terry, and I think we both felt that's an important question. I don't know that either of us is prepared to answer it. It's something that I've realized I'm going to have to incorporate into future thinking about nature and writing. I don't know what shape that's going to take, but I did want to state that something is there which is incumbent upon any writer—but writers about nature, maybe, in particular—to think about. How does that fact of our time change the way we can look at and feel about and respond to the natural world when it, too, is vulnerable to total change?

WILLIAMS: You know, Bob, the fact that we do have the power now to destroy everything is the darkest side. Call it the "down side of the sacred." The other side of that—it's like the yin-yang—is that we also now have the capabilities because of the vision of "Earth-rise," because of what we now know, of becoming one world, one culture. And so we are in that transitionary state of developing a new mythology. No one can predict what that will be. All we can ask of ourselves is to be fiercely attentive toward our personal gestures and rituals and the stories we tell to create that sense of wholeness. Of what is most trustworthy in our lives.

FINCH: I agree. I think it's going to take an effort of imagination, individually and communally, commensurate with what it took to create the old myths. It's just going to take that kind of an effort, and it's in that belief that I find my justification for what I do. And I think that you do, too.

WILLIAMS: Yes. I feel the same.

LUEDERS: May we enlarge the dialogue now by inviting questions from the audience?

QUESTION: One of you said earlier this evening, in describing the process that you use, that you go out to discover, to learn, and to serve. Could you explain ways in which you see your work as service?

WILLIAMS: I think I actually was the one who said "to serve." And I didn't mean that my writing is an act of service at all. I think that would be quite presumptuous. What I meant was that you are attentive, that you pay attention to the world that you are a part of, and that, as a writer, somehow you try to make sense of what you see, with the acknowledgment that it's only really a personal vision. I mean, it's just one way of seeing. If you are in the service of something, you are receptive, open, you are a student. It depends on a frank awareness of how little you know. You realize you are in the service or attendance of something so much larger than yourself.

FINCH: I'm not sure I have a lot to say about that. What it brings to my mind is a question of what purpose people like us serve, or of what use is the kind of writing we do. And all I can think of is a review of my last book that was in the *Yankee Magazine* with another book of nature writing by a woman in Maine. Both books describe some of the more peculiar or embarrassing situations we got ourselves into. The heading of the review, which I thought was rather nice, called us "Useful Fools."

QUESTION: Mr. Finch, I'm not quite sure I got the full picture when you were talking about the other writer, your friend who viewed the world as an atomic grid. I thought you implied, because it was an atomic grid, that nature writers should then look at the whole world rather than putting their efforts and perspective into their own personal little one area of the grid. I think that if each of you is writing within your own grid, with all of your parallel cultures and with all of your parallel writers, you are going to cover the world anyway.

And just because we now have a world problem, we shouldn't devoid our efforts of looking at our own individual natural areas.

FINCH: Well, I probably didn't get it across very clearly. I don't think he meant that we should be writing about the global environment rather than the local environment. There are people who do that in different ways. I don't know that anybody could know the global environment in the way that we are talking about knowing a landscape. The point of this essay I have been referring to, if I could restate it a little bit, is that, by and large, we have in the past looked upon nature as something fundamentally outside of human tampering which we can use as a refuge — from ourselves, really, and from our mistakes, and also as a testing ground for ourselves. It seems to me that we're a species that naturally learns by trial and error, and we've done that. Consciously or unconsciously we've always counted upon the Earth to be our tolerant parent and let us make mistakes and slap us when we went too far off so eventually we'd learn the right thing to do. As we've grown in scale and technology, our mistakes have become more and more costly. And now there are environmental processes that we've tampered with which may have mortal effects on some of the basic systems.

Terrence Des Pres was really using the nuclear threat, I think, as the metaphor for that ultimate tampering. Not that we can't do equally bad things gradually, but this would be an instant wiping out of things. And we can't look on nature as our savior any more in that old sense, as a savior from ourselves, from our own mistakes. In fact, it can't be a testing ground any more for us. We have to imagine what we can no longer afford to actually try out. We have to imagine ourselves as part of the Earth rather than acting as if we weren't and finding out too late that we are. And that is how I get back to the value of what I feel I do. Because what Terry does and what I do and what other writers do, I think, are in a very real sense acts of the imagination, and that becomes more and more important in an age like ours. We have to imagine the truth; we can't try it out.

WILLIAMS: You bring to mind this business of bio-regionalism — the importance of knowing one place well, of knowing our own homeland well so that we take on our own responsibility, our own accountability of where we live. We must become biologically literate, so that we know the migrating species of birds, we know native grasses and plants, we know where our water comes from and where our waste goes, so that we no longer need these visions of UFOs coming in and saving us. We actually have to look to ourselves. I think this nuclear age demands that we change our ideas about ourselves, that we, in fact, yes, see the Earth floating in space, but by the same token we recognize our home, our family, our community, and therefore become fiercely accountable for the landscape that we are a part of. We can begin to adopt an ethics of place.

QUESTIONER: I would agree with that one hundred per cent and say we should carry it over so that we recognize that the other cultures are there. We are so isolated in our thinking at times and don't give credence to what's going on in the other areas.

WILLIAMS: And I think that's vital to the whole idea of diversity, which the land celebrates and depends upon.

FINCH: That's exactly the point I was going to make. The discoveries of an ecological point of view—I mean, the scientific discoveries or the recognition of things which were often realized instinctively by cultures closer to the land—give us leads in other aspects of our lives. What's now become the ecological cliché that diversity creates stability of an environment can be applied to human cultures as well.

WILLIAMS: And, in my mind, that's what this business of empathy is—in the most profound sense.

FINCH: You know, I find one thing missing in what we've been saying. Maybe it's been implicit but I want to make it explicit. There is an awful lot of emphasis in talking about the writing that we do, about responsibility, discovering what's important, learning right behavior and so on. In my experience, education can go a long way, but I don't think it's enough. There has to be joy in what you do, if it's going to be self-perpetuating. One impetus in all of my writing is that I feel I have to convey a sense of joy in what I'm doing and finding out, or else whatever lesson there may be in it is not going to grab hold. I have to celebrate in some way in everything I do so that it doesn't just become a moral imperative: "Yes, this is what we

should do—this is how we should manage our land and our resources."
Pragmatic and moral obligations aren't enough. I don't think that
will save us. We actually have to find a more rewarding way of living in the way we look at the land.

LUEDERS: May I suggest that in addition to studying natural history—compiling, discovering, and utilizing all of the elements that
the advance of science opens to us—writing natural history, to revert
to the title of our series, humanizes all of the rest. It gives human
dimension to what otherwise can tend to dehumanize the very knowledge which is the basis of our advance into the possibilities of the
world ahead of us in an atomic age.

I hope you will allow that to be something like a wrap-up
statement. We've run the clock around to close to an hour and a
half. Further conversation will be, I trust, not only possible but
inevitable, stimulated by the dialogue we've just shared with these
two authors. [applause]

WILLIAMS: What we really need right now is a closing ritual . . .
something to bind us beyond these words. [more applause]

Dialogue Three

FIELD NOTES AND THE LITERARY PROCESS

Gary Paul Nabhan
and Ann Zwinger

February 15, 1988

GARY PAUL NABHAN, Ph.D., is co-founder of Native Seeds—SEARCH, a nonprofit organization that conserves native crops and their wild relatives. He is Assistant Director for Research at the Desert Botanical Garden in Phoenix, Arizona. In 1985, Dr. Nabhan received the John Burroughs Medal for *Gathering the Desert*. He is also the author of *The Desert Smells Like Rain—a Naturalist in Papago Indian Country*; *Saguaro*; and *Enduring Seeds*. His technical research has been published in botany, anthropology, horticulture, geography, and nutrition journals and books in five countries.

ANN HAYMOND ZWINGER, nature writer and illustrator, is the author of widely acclaimed books, including *Beyond the Aspen Grove*; *Land Above the Trees*; *A Conscious Stillness*, with Edwin Way Teale; *Wind in the Rock*; and *A Desert Country Near the Sea*. In 1975 she received the John Burroughs Medal for *Run, River, Run*. She serves as director of the Colorado chapter of the Nature Conservancy. Her latest book is *This Mysterious Land: The Four Deserts of North America*.

LUEDERS: Welcome once again. We're pleased that all of you can help us celebrate Presidents' Day in the Fine Arts Museum Auditorium by sharing a conversation between two recipients of the John Burroughs Medal as authors of natural history, Ann Zwinger and Gary Paul Nabhan.

I'm going to start the dialogue by asking a very broad question about what it is you two wish to do as writers of natural history and how you go about doing it. I know that you are both extremely disciplined writers — that you don't squeeze the imagination out of your writing by any means, but that the procedure is a long, difficult, demanding one. And, on that note, Gary, can you begin by telling us what is it you do?

NABHAN: A good question. For the last twelve years, I've used a little poem as my statement of work. It was first printed in *High Country News* a while back. That was when *HCN* was based in the environmental publishing capital of the western world, Lander, Wyoming. The poem is called, "Terra Incognita," or "Earth Undiscovered."

> I work with tumbleweeds and dust,
> Telling people we've come the wrong way.
> This land has never been pictured.
> Get inside the wind, you'll see.
> It moves too fast, it moves too slow,
> You can never keep up with it.
> If you're dying to, not just if you want to,
> Take on the tone and age of bones,
> Get as hard as them,
> As hard as parched corn,
> While singing
> "Time and time and time again,
> Time again we've lost our way."
> Those of us remaining here

Know that good directions are hard to come by.
We assume the way Terra gives,
What she breathes into us,
Molds out of clay.
Like earthenware, Terra holds us, preserves us.
A bit of her taste rubs off on us.
She gives us a trailing scent to follow.

I believe like most kinds of writers we're simply trying to find our way along the earth. Perhaps, as naturalists, we use indicator plants to guide us along or follow the way the land itself is shaped. We read the landscape as a reflection of our own spiritual journey. We immerse ourselves in this world, by crawling inside another creature's skin, binding ourselves to a piece of land for a few years, or maybe immersing ourselves within a rural culture. That is a process of grounding, but it is also the best way for me to get on with the writing process.

For my book *Gathering the Desert*, I tried some naturalistic "method acting." For each of the twelve plants that was in the book, I tried to live awhile entirely in its atmosphere, consuming its plant products, smelling it twenty-four hours a day, doing whatever I could to absorb the plant's ambience so that I could write about it. For a plant like the *Washingtonia* palm in the desert oases, this approach was delightful. I harvested the little palm fruit — they're quite small compared to the size of a date — and would eat them while I was writing. I slept under the palm trees and heard the wind in the fronds all night. While traveling between palm oases, I'd chug down date shakes and wear a palm hat.

The stakes were raised when I came to the wild chile chapter, "The Red Hot Mother of Chiles." [laughter] I popped wild chiles constantly. Once you get chile on your hands, there are some things that you really can't do without feeling pain. After weeks of drinking mescal while writing the agave chapter, I finally ran through all of the bootleg mescal smuggled into this country from Sonora. And then there were the side effects from writing the bean chapter. [more laughter] If you've ever noticed the labels on those tin cans of beans, it doesn't say, "wife-pleasing beans" — it says, "husband-pleasing beans," and that's about all they please.

And so, each chapter became an attempt to discover the character of a particular plant and its effects on humankind over the ages. You can judge whether it worked or not. For me, it was a worthwhile exercise in that it made me realize how plants form the basis of our lives—our food, our shelter, our habitat, nearly everything that we have around us. We are also indebted to a number of animals that, through co-evolution, shaped those plants. In other words, the plant foods we eat each day are really designed to some degree by the seed dispersers or the pollinators that have co-evolved with those plants.

One can ask the question: What good is nature writing? For instance, does it really "help" the plants I write about? In some cases, one can write about endangered plants and, because of the demand it creates for them among hobbyist-collectors, they are gone the next day. The same thing can obviously happen to a favorite place, if one's writing attracts too many tourists to it. There are some writers who now take great pains to change the names and the directions to places so that other people can't get there. If we ask, "Does nature writing help conserve the organisms and habitats that we write about?" I believe that few of us can make great claims to successful conservation through writing alone. Well, then, does it help humankind? Paul Brooks has argued that, historically, great naturalists have shaped public opinion and that wilderness writing has given the American mind a distinctive identity. People like Muir, Thoreau, Roosevelt, and Burroughs in some ways have influenced the whole destiny of this country. And yet, most of us who write natural history have a small readership. I feel, when I write, I am writing for myself or for friends like many of you. We are a modest-sized group of individuals. Who or what, then, does nature writing help? I think it helps each of us as individuals gain perspective on the "external" world. We need to balance the internal with the external. A focus on something other than ourselves is probably healthy in this society, because we are so consumed with ourselves. Fiction writing, movies, and music are all going the other direction; they become more and more self-indulgent and human-centered, rather than reaching out to wider and wider circles.

Recently, I came upon this wonderful Robinson Jeffers quote from 1941: "The whole human race spends too much emotion on itself. The happiest and freest man is the scientist investigating nature or the artist admiring it, the person who is interested in things that are not human. Or if he is interested in human beings, let him regard them objectively as a small part of the great music. Certainly humanity has its claims on all of us. We can best fulfill them by keeping our emotional sanity, and this by seeing around and beyond the human race." I sense that the daily act of observing nature, writing about it and internalizing it, offers this kind of cure.

So the bottom line for me is that I am not writing primarily to *save* the world, but to fit into it more fully. I am writing, perhaps, for some health that I can gain through this grounding process. Perhaps it is like the whale or bat echo-locating, or the bowerbird constructing a beautiful platform of plants to announce its territory. Perhaps I write to affirm the relationship between my home and my identity.

LUEDERS: Gary, as an ethnobotanist, you cultivate the tone of both the exterior world of nature and the interior world of a culture. And we might return to that later. I noticed that you included cultures in your sense of nature writing along with their indigenous plant life.

Most "nature writers," in my observation, are a little uncomfortable with that title. I think that's often because they're so individual and because they bring more than one point of view to bear on their work, as you do in your ethnobotany. Ann Zwinger does this as an artist, with a background in art history, as well as being a naturalist and a writer who deals with the natural world in her own distinctive way. Ann, what would you like to tell us about that distinctive way?

ZWINGER: After hearing Gary, I've completely revised what I was going to say. I think we *are* out to save the world—in a very quiet, minor way. Nature writers, I think, are saying, "Look at this best of all possible worlds." My theory is that we should try to get the reader to really *look* at the natural world. If you once look at something, really *see* it, ask a question about it, get an answer, learn something about it, it becomes yours. And once it becomes yours, you'll never destroy it. I think that's one thing that nature writers do. Maybe that's hopelessly idealistic, because I certainly have long since given up the thought that anybody's going to change the world—least of all me. But there is a sense in nature writing of writing for nature, and there is a great comfort in that and a sense of home.

LUEDERS: And yet you spend so much of your time as a nature writer in the field, away from home.

ZWINGER: But that's home. That's *really* home. I had occasion to go through all my books lately and the thread that runs through is an expanding sense of home. I began writing about a place in the mountains that we owned, which was easy of access, just fifty minutes away from Colorado Springs. If you ran out of milk you could get in the car and go ten miles to Woodland Park and get a carton. With each book the circle has widened.

The Cabeza Prieta, where I went while working on a book on American deserts, is about as far out as you can get. There you sit for a week, under 110-degree heat, counting sheep—in the daytime yet. I mean, come on, folks, you have to be a little bit dotty to do that! But that miserable, creaky blind that housed between the ceiling and the metal corrugated roof the nest of a handsome wood rat became "home." I enjoyed my own ground squirrel, was visited by my own whiptail lizard, and my own bighorn sheep came and watched me while they munched mesquite pods. We co-existed, and that was home.

Maybe that's what nature writers do: they write about home—and supposedly you don't mess up your home. And maybe we're saying we can acclimate to this world that seems so alien to so many, the natural world that we've built walls against. I have a friend whose idea of roughing it is when the color television is out at the Marriott—and *that's* my audience. If I can say to somebody like that, "There is something real and vital and exciting out there," catch their attention, pique their interest, nudge their curiosity, that's the audience I want to reach. Bless you for being here and for reading what we write, but we're already on the same side. I want to reach somebody who isn't, who's never been there, who's never stumbled across an evening primrose, never held its bud in his hand one summer evening and felt it open. I want to find somebody who can look at a Devil's Hole pupfish and think, what a miracle that it's still there. I want to find somebody who is angry about "these damned environmentalists." I want to find somebody who's not a believer.

And there are all kinds of ways of making people aware of and at home in the natural world. One of the things I do is to go as a consultant on San Juan River trips. I just love the people who come out, and the first thing they say about the river is "Yuck," because the river is brown and there are no trees. And I just smile sweetly, because I know at the end of being outdoors for five days they're going to come to a different dialogue with the outdoors, and it's going to make a difference. And by the end, they *do* love it. Maybe they're not going to go home and read natural history and maybe they're not going to go home and join the Nature Conservancy. But somewhere along the way a question is going to come up and they're going to step across the line they never stepped across before and say, "It's important we don't put that dam there."

NABHAN: I agree with you in the sense that the key thing is getting people to make their own primary observations, to see that beauty firsthand. Paul Sears said it, I think, this way: We seldom save anything we haven't yet learned to love. I think that the key is encouraging people to make firsthand observations of the world around them, because if we take the time to look and listen rather than assume we know what's around us, our world view will radically change. We walk through the world with blinders on. And the trick of nature writing is to stimulate the reader to put the book down, to go out and make his or her own original discoveries about a place.

ZWINGER: Well, that's why we're here tonight, and I've been waiting all day to hear how you take notes. See, the last time I saw Gary, he was up to his knees under a truck out in the Cabeza Prieta trying to dig us out. And he *wasn't* taking notes. He was saving three damsels in distress. But this was one of the things that intrigued me about our dialogue this evening, because I think we may come at it so differently that I'm curious to hear.

LUEDERS: Let's talk about the nuts and bolts of writing natural history. A great deal of the work — most of it, perhaps — takes place in the field, first of all. That's where you live, so to speak, where you say your home is. I accept that, but it isn't easy when you look so chic here tonight, Ann. And we find Gary Nabhan here with a tie on . . .

ZWINGER: This is the way I dress in the field, my dear. I mean, doesn't everybody? [laughter]

NABHAN: This is what I wear when I jack up jeeps in sand, too. [more laughter]

LUEDERS: But we keep in tune with the natural world one way or another. I'm looking right past Gary now at our one prop. Those of you who have been following the series will appreciate the fact that Terry Tempest Williams is giving us some background cue for each dialogue by whatever she has put in the flower pot on the end table. This time it's a cactus.

ZWINGER: Is she saying that you have two prickly authors?

LUEDERS: Maybe. But it's a very special cactus, and it does take us out into the field and it does suggest that what we're doing here tonight is pretty well bred for the kinds of things that you do in the field. A lot of the note taking, a lot of what happens in that first-hand relationship with your home, is what gets distilled eventually into the books that take us where you have been and let us see through your eyes, as the authors, what you have seen. What is that process? Where are the nuts and bolts, and how do they fit together? Would you both talk about this?

NABHAN: Ann and I have a running controversy about whether artists and scientists really work in the same way. Ann was trained in art history and I was trained as a biologist, and so perhaps we see the world from different angles because each of those traditions has its own particular rigor in the way it observes the world. Perhaps it is a matter of emphasizing the right side of the brain over the left side of the brain and vice versa. However, my own opinion is that the act of scientific discovery is *not* much different from artistic discovery. The kind of "Eureka!" moment that I *want* to record in my notebook isn't too different from what Ann experiences as an artist. The creative process has been found to be much the same in the sciences as it is in the arts. In other words, when we notice something new that we haven't encountered before, it is because we've jarred ourselves out of our normal world view. We've thrown ourselves into the chaos of Cabeza Prieta or wherever, and then discovered a greater pattern. I believe that that moment — the "Eureka!" moment — is at the root of most scientific advances, as it is for most art and for nature writing.

After that moment of discovery, scientists and artists take different routes. A scientist then spends three or four years taking meticulous data to prove the creative hypothesis that he came upon in the middle of the night out in the wilderness. The same kind of creative flash may happen to Ann, but she follows it with hours of precise work with pen and ink, using her craft to polish that raw gem into a work of art. At the onset she has to open herself up to discovery in the same way a scientist does. Scientists sometimes hide behind the "scientific method." But that's not the whole story. Philosophers of science can't explain to us why a scientist comes upon that unique insight or hypothesis which makes him or her *want* to take data on some phenomenon. The scientist's end product may reside in a technical journal in very stilted language, but the moment of discovery experienced earlier is probably the same for artists, poets, naturalists, and scientists.

Look at the kind of creative minds that we now have writing about their field science — E. O. Wilson, Dan Janzen, Adrian Forsyth, Roger Swain, John Janovy, Wes Jackson, Richard Nelson, and David Quammen. They are writers trained in science, who constantly throw themselves back into the chaos or unknown of this planet and come up with novel hypotheses and observations. It makes good nature writing, at one level, but it takes five to ten more years to shape into a neat, tidy little story that a scientific journal would publish. The great advantage of nature writing is that it focuses on that process of discovery rather than on the six following years of measurements with meter tapes, bomb calorimeters, aerial photos, or infrared thermometers that would bore us all to tears. What I highlight in my journal is what I haven't seen before. Watching carefully, I pay attention to the phenomenology of a process or behavior, watching every step of it as it happens, and trying to record it in detail sufficient enough to see if there are any contradictions between it and any preconceived theory.

Let me give an example, because that all sounds dreadfully abstract. When I was interested in wild chiles, something clicked when an old Pima Indian man in Sonora said they are called "bird peppers" because birds with red feathers disperse them. I then talked to an ornithologist who suggested that certain birds may need the carotene in red chiles and other red or yellow fruits to keep their plumage colorful for mating displays. I began to think about the dispersal syndrome of the wild chiles, so that when I returned into the field, I looked where chiles were growing. They usually grow under the canopies of red-berried trees, perhaps mimicking the red berries that cardinals and finches regularly consume. Chiles are shrubs that need some kind of protection to keep them from being killed by frosts. But rather than being sheltered under the dominant cover plants in the vegetation, whether it was mesquite or oak, the chiles were established largely under red-fruited trees where the birds had dispersed them. A bird picks up a chile while foraging for other berries, and drops it or defecates it out under the trees where it spends most of its time feeding, thereby offering protection to a chile seeding later on.

These discoveries took very little time. But to verify this beautiful pattern, I am now doing a whole battery of measurements in wild vegetation where these chiles grow. I have also set up some experiments where I have wild chiles under mesquite, wild chiles under red-fruited shrubs, wild chiles in the open — and will hopefully observe which birds come to them and where they send their seeds. This sort of scientific verification may take another four or five years to complete. But the discovery of the connection between the "bird pepper" folk name, the dispersal syndrome, and the chile's habitat preferences happened while I was writing my nature book, not while I was looking for a hypothesis to submit to the National Science Foundation.

ZWINGER: Wow! That is a whole background that you have that I do not have, so I come at it from a different direction. And that's just pure observation, with maybe a lot of tricks of the trade of how to look that I've learned as an art historian — the best training for being a nature writer I could ever have asked for. You learn in the western tradition to read from left to right. We have a very specific way of looking at the world. And all the skills that I learned as an art historian, the visual skills, are the ones that I rely on in taking field notes.

I have none of the ballast of scientific background which gives your work such authority. For that I depend on somebody like you, Gary. I come home with all the questions; then I need to go find somebody who has the answers. So, in a sense, you are doing the primary research, and I depend upon that primary research that scientists do for what I'm writing about.

NABHAN: Oh, I'm not going to let you get away with that, because your own field research is valid, too. I maintain that the primary

observations which you have recorded will interest some scientist
ten years from now when he reads your Cape region book and says,
"Damn, why is this plant growing with that plant?" or "What was
that bird doing there at that time of year?" Because you've accu-
rately recorded the biotic community of a particular place, any scientist can use your notes or books as benchmarks. It's because you
truly paint a landscape of what you saw at a particular moment that
future scientists can compare their snapshots with yours, or use
your observations to guide an inquiry that we can't even imagine at
this time.

ZWINGER: Well, be that as it may—that idea brings to mind one of
the things Edwin Way Teale, who to my mind was the quintessen-
tial nature writer, said, which seems to me so true—that nature
writing is preserving a time and a place as a fly is preserved in
amber, with every bristle and hair and wing vein intact. Nature
writing does preserve a place—maybe more poignantly for the writer,
but also, I trust, for the reader.

When you take field notes, there are a lot of devices that I
think you use to observe well. I'll bet Gary does, and I certainly
sketch in the margin of the page, which provides a wonderful backup.
You consciously call on all six senses; you have a way of ticking
them off in your mind: What does it smell like? What does it look
like?

Again, I remember Edwin Way Teale who quoted William
Beebe as saying, "When I'm out in the field taking notes, I stop and
think, when I'm back at my desk, what are the questions that I'm
going to be asking and I'm going to wish I had the answers to?"
And that helps me. But then, there is the terrible time that you get
back and you realize you missed something vital and are unable to
get back there again. What do you do, Gary? Do you have any
solutions?

NABHAN: Well, I depend upon all senses when I'm out there. Unless
I do, when I get back to a cozy room with my notebook or a word
processor to write something up in essay form, I won't be able to
remember the sounds that were there, or what the light was like.
When I take a lot of notes in the field, there is a chance that some of
the sounds I hear in that landscape will carry over into the sounds
of the words I use to describe a place. I work hard on that because

I can't do that again later. Recording the weather is also important. I feel I have failed when I read a journal entry and I can't even tell whether it was raining on me at the time other than that the ink is smeared . . .

ZWINGER: That's why I use a pencil.

NABHAN: . . . and that it could be that I simply spilled a beer on my notebook — that it has nothing to do with the weather. The point is that there are some features of a landscape that you can't retrace later on. Bird songs, waves crashing, leaves rustling — all of these things serve as prompts for me when I'm reworking a field journal, particularly for something that I want to use later on as raw material for an essay. It's the sensory data that I want to record in detail — so that it prompts me as soon as I read it to reexperience a particular moment.

ZWINGER: I would like to know if something that happens to me also happens to you, and if it happens to anybody else in this room: are there times when you've been out, and whether you've taken notes or not, later and under certain circumstances, it all comes back full blown, in wonderful and exhilarating detail? I think it happens for me when I'm sitting at the word processor, because I'm focusing intently and remembering intensely. I can close my eyes and walk it through and, in a very peculiar way, it comes back, filtered through time and absence and distance, with great glowing clarity.

I suspect it's something we *can* learn to do. That mental gear-shift has served me well — for instance, in working on the Baja book there were places I knew I'd never get to again. There were times when I may have been a little sloppy in note taking — or when a truck is going up and down like this [gesture], your handwriting goes to hell in a handbasket. You must be able to store a lot, be able to discipline yourself, to have made mental notes, to trust in the back of your head, and to keep saying to yourself, "Oh please, when I get home, *be* there." And then, miraculously, it is. You've got to believe it does work, yet I can't explain it — do either of you, as writers, do this too?

LUEDERS: It's strange that so many people nowadays depend on a camera or a tape recorder — chiefly that visual tool of the camera —

to do this, and it doesn't altogether serve, does it? It somehow has to boil down in different terms than you get from that photographic reproduction. You have to find some salient feature which comes through the other senses, or a combination of the senses. One of the things in that boiling down is olfactory — the sense of smell, which is so often left out of our recounting of experience. And both of you use it to such good effect. Frequently it is the very best means by which you can call back from some distant time or place what happened, what was total in that previous experience.

ZWINGER: You know, our sense of smell is a very primitive sense; and, if there's one thing that's frustrating to write about, it's what something smells like. Do you realize the only way you can describe smells is to say it smells *like* . . . ? There is no precise primary vocabulary. There are desert plants that have this evocative, resinous, clean, sharp smell. Once you've smelled it, you know what it is. But I've just sweated blood trying to describe the odors of desert plants. The group as a whole seems to me distinctive in smell.

NABHAN: That's why we call it the hot, stinking desert. [laughter]

LUEDERS: The desert smells like rain, to quote one of our authors.

NABHAN: That's why I want to be the first author of an adult scratch-and-sniff book about the desert. [laughter] If we could just have these things on the inside of the cover where you . . .

ZWINGER: I'll buy a dozen. That's neat.

LUEDERS: As an artist, Ann, you must be drawn into the visual; and in reproducing plants, which you do in your delicate and yet firm line drawings, you must feel the absence of color. Or am I supposing something that isn't a problem for you?

ZWINGER: I don't think about it. And let me clarify — I'm an illustrator, not an artist. I choose to work in a very confined way, and I'm not sure that you can be an artist and a writer at the same time. I have a very talented daughter who is constantly torn because of this. I think each discipline is too consuming. For me, illustration is secondary to writing. Sometimes I think of chucking all the writing and being an artist, and it scares the wits out of me — it's scary in a way writing is not. I mean, writing is miserable, dirty stuff — we all know that — but it's not as much an act of courage as being an artist, possibly because a writer begins with a craft about which the public has a general understanding. I don't think artists enjoy this. Some day I just might do it — I think about it a lot.

But illustrating is a back-and-forth activity. Gary talks about this, too. You look at something, like a living plant, and you see all you can. Then you read about it as a plant and learn what its peculiar situation is, and when you go back to that plant, you see it with new eyes. It's this constant back and forth that is so helpful.

NABHAN: I agree. At first I didn't recognize the significance of all those desert smells. Then I learned about how resins, oils, and waxes control transpiration from the leaves of desert plants. Plants during a long drought just keep on secreting more and more of their oils or waxes to slow down water loss. Once a rain hits them, there is an incredible flush of volatile oils released into the air. After I learned that, I began to crawl around on my knees to smell other plants that I hadn't paid attention to before.

LUEDERS: May we follow your field notes and journal materials into your workshop at home and trace the writing process that each of you goes through once you are back at that screen? Each of you uses a word processor, I take it from your earlier remarks. So you now have the process of taking this raw material and fashioning it into the books which reach us and give us the delight and the firmness of your observations together with some sense of the whole — the process leading us through a whole book rather than simply stopping us in one place. What's involved for you in this?

ZWINGER: I *try* to transcribe my field notes as soon as possible, even though that's not always possible. I transcribe them directly — mess, misspelling, I don't care, it doesn't matter. I just need to get them into the computer while things are fresh in my head. This is one of the times I keep my eyes shut a lot, hoping to visualize, to bring back the whole gorgeous array of what I've seen.

Also, along the way, I have been taking notes assiduously, may have, say, twelve cases of note cards, of research. It's like writing a term paper — writing for me is somehow putting these two basic elements of research and personal experience together. We were speaking today in Ed's writing class about writing outlines. I am constitutionally incapable of writing an outline, which says I must have a pretty messy mind.

So I've got field notes, and I've got note cards. I have a helper whom I would pay anything to file note cards. I mean, she could retire to Spain on what I would pay her to file note cards. It's like playing Concentration — only instead of fifty-two cards, you've got 52,000 to call back to mind. From that mishmash you write a rough draft. I must admit that when faced with a first draft I clean closets, scrub sinks, and watch a lot of Bronco football to avoid writing a rough draft. I watch so much football I discovered that the "fullback" hadn't just eaten a big dinner, that the "halfback" was really all there, and that the "quarterback" was John Elway. [laughter] But there comes a time when I can't put it off . . . [the laughter continues] I'm delighted. We should do more one liners, Gary.

NABHAN: We should watch football more together. [more laughter]

ZWINGER: Ideally, I would like to come back with a sheaf of good field notes, take all those note cards, apply the seat of the pants to the seat of the chair for a few weeks, and put it all together right then and there. But there is just too much material, and it's such a *miserable* job. It's worse than cleaning public rest rooms. But I get things together in hunks and feed those into the field notes, which you can do easily on the computer.

I wish I had a program that would allow me to store and sort, a way of going directly from notes on a hard disk into manuscript, because I still type the notes out, run them off on regular-size paper, and then cut them into three- by five-inch cards. I still want to play Concentration with them. And maybe (I console myself) a lot of learning of unfamiliar material goes on during typing notes. For instance, when you read an article on kangaroo rats, you may also pick up three note cards on kangaroo mice — the food that they are eating and so on and so forth — and to have the mobility of note cards, you make several copies of that so that you can use one article in a lot of different ways. I go bananas trying to get all of this together — it's pure donkey work. Anybody can write a rough draft, if their mind is weak enough and their back is strong enough and they can stand orange letters on the screen. And I may come up with five hundred pages of complete dross. I mean, I am amazed at the ease and grace with which I can write badly. When I taught a nature writing course at Colorado College last fall, we all stood up, raised our right hands, and said, "I give myself permission to write absolute garbage. I cannot be perfect every day. Every other day, maybe. But not every day." There was a great release in that for me — I hope it was for the students, too. Because you think you have these incredibly marvelous ideas and you spew out this fantastic prose, then you read it the next day, and you know it's unremittingly bad. It's important to go on from there and not lose your impetus.

Still, it's downhill from the first draft on, once you get out of the field notes and note cards and have hard copy. I travel a lot. I get on the airplane with my manuscript, and I am as happy as a tick in sheep country. To me, it's the editing process that is the elegance of writing. That's when you play, dance, sing with words, sometimes even gallop to the wind. The editing process — the refining, the thinking, the letting your mind play with connections, cutting — is the exhilarating part of writing. It's as if you're making a beautiful stock and you've put all the good things in it, and you take it off the stove and it tastes fair. But if you boil it down to a third, it gains in intensity, it gains in flavor, it gains something ineffable.

I'm convinced that we all work too hard. There is this wonderful reservoir in the back of your head that will take over, and marvelous things will happen if you just let them. I think a lot of writing comes from that. And it's from having lived, breathed, slept, loathed, hated, loved, giggled over, despaired over a manuscript for a long period of time — of being totally possessed, of even knowing the precise page where a certain subject resides — that the ideas come and sort themselves through, that synthesis occurs. I feel as if I am being a kind of amanuensis to all this. Sometimes it's almost like automatic writing when the book itself takes over and tells you how it should be written, when the book now has a life of its own.

NABHAN: Just put the word processor into overdrive.

ZWINGER: Right. Floor it.

NABHAN: I do things a lot differently, because I have *green* letters on my screen. [laughter]

ZWINGER: And your typewriter keys look red when you finish. [more laughter]

NABHAN: My field notes begin as random observations, not consciously linked by a preconceived theme. At that moment, I don't try to write essay fragments for later polishing. When I am spending a lot of time in the field, it limits my imagination if I record only material related to one theme or intent. But some things intrigue me more than others, and they gather momentum. So most of my field notes aren't done explicitly for essay writing later on; they're just general habit. The same thing is true with some of my science reading. When I start to shape an essay, I'll brood over it and read about the topic or tangents to that topic.

Recently, I broke away from years of botany writing to work on an essay about why domestic turkeys are so dumb. I read everything I could about turkeys, from the 1888 *Standards of Perfection* for poultry breeds to a wonderful paper by Aldo Starker Leopold on the nature of wildness in turkeys. Then I observed turkeys. I went up to Canyon de Chelly and looked at turkey petroglyphs. I looked at a prehistoric turkey effigy. When people died in Anasazi times, a turkey was sacrificed with them, a corn cob shoved down its throat, the turkey was beheaded, and it was then buried with them. I immersed myself in stacks of references on turkey biology, archeology, and domestication. Then, I shoved all the references and notes back into the file drawer and started writing. As a scientist, I'm so preoccupied about facts in technical literature that to switch over to writing I almost have to say, "Okay, I'm not going to load myself down with all this on my desk or it will bury the narrative." Instead, I see what I've retained from my notes and readings that won't go away that I can explain to my mother or to my five-year-old boy, so that a particular image becomes real to them. After I write the first draft, I pull out all the references and see whether I've correctly interpreted them. In other words, what have I learned that's lasting enough in my own mind to be able to articulate it clearly? I think a lot of scientists have to do that. To get loose enough to engage the general public in what interests us, we have to take an antidote to cure the billions of facts that we stuff in our heads.

The other metaphor that I use is that an essay is an ecosystem — it's not a linear sequence, it has energy flows and nutrients and lives in it that are more than a listing of facts. It is a mosaic of images, and people remember images. I can go from one part of an essay to another and juxtapose two images in the last few lines of one paragraph and the first few lines of another. That creates some kind of connection, or perhaps a tension, from which the next part follows. An essay is obviously linear in the sense that you read fifteen pages from one through fifteen, but you can plant an image in part two that flowers in part four, and introduce its pollinator in part one. Between various sections of an essay, I try to create a certain tension. And, again, I think it's those juxtapositions that force us to think about the world in a different way.

ZWINGER: Oh, I agree. It's seeing an old world in new ways and a new world in old ways. Because, as you say, you're taking a lot of field notes that are really for scientific purposes, and yet you're so good that you can go back and use those as a nature writer.

NABHAN: If you discipline yourself right. Ann, you've dealt with old naturalists' field notes and you know which ones you gain something from, which ones are both literate and useful when you're visiting a place. And I think that's one motivation for what I do. I've read old naturalists' field notes, particularly on vegetation change, that greatly interest me. So when I write, I sometimes think, "How can I describe this place in my field notes so that a hundred years from now a botanist visiting the same place will be able to discern if anything has changed?" That takes a fair amount of detail that may not be immediately valuable to me. However, I know that I've greatly valued the explorers and travelers and naturalists before me who have maintained that kind of detail in their journals, and would like to reciprocate.

ZWINGER: God bless John Xantus.

NABHAN: Right. Right. Exactly. Or Carl Lumholtz or Forrest Shreve. They are capturing a time and a place that's gone, too. And what we need is to remind ourselves how rapidly that happens and how pervasively it happens, that places which used to be grasslands are now creosote flats, and some people assume that they have always been deserts.

ZWINGER: Back to the field notes—I think there is a certain tactile satisfaction in taking field notes by hand. I've been contemplating getting a portable computer, but I really have mixed feelings about it. Because I think that there is that wonderful sensual feeling of pencil on paper—and the connection between the eye, the head, the shoulder, the elbow, the wrist, the hand, the pencil, the paper— that really makes taking field notes something unique.

It's like collecting art. A lot of people collect paintings, which have been well thought through. They are the culmination of a long train of thought, a solution to a visual problem. That's what a book is. But if I had all the money in the world and could collect anything I wanted, I would collect sketches and drawings because they're like field notes. They're rough, but the true person is there, and the intent. Notes are the right-now, the what-you-see-is-what-you-get. There's nothing in between artist and observer, no sophistication, no thought of presenting your best face to the world. They are the intimate records of personality.

LUEDERS: And the immediacy.

ZWINGER: And the immediacy. And that to me is the exciting part— not the big finished work. Maybe I'm saying I think it's more fun to write field notes than to write books. [Pause]

LUEDERS: It's more fun to talk like this than to have speeches to give or to prepare too much outline before we have such conversations. I hope you agree, and I'm pleased that you've followed the line of the dialogue the way you have. I wonder if it isn't time to invite the audience in to see if they might direct us in the rest of our remarks. Are there questions that you would like to put to either or both of our authors?

QUESTION: This is a question about the field notes and the writing. You talked a lot about writing at home or in your study as the time when you really process and put it all together, and I was wondering if there is a time when you are doing field notes, when you're out there experiencing what is so memorable to you, that metaphor and meaning and wonderment actually happens on the spot and that you do write that—because you talked about the senses, smell and sight, the primary senses. But does the other happen out there as well as inside at your writing desk?

NABHAN: That's where it happens. That's where you're in the naturalist's trance, and the new discovery happens.

ZWINGER: Absolutely.

QUESTIONER: Are you able to transcribe that occasionally — or often — or do you try to hit that in your field notes? Or is it that you want to just write enough to be able to get back to that in your mind later?

ZWINGER: All of the above. Taking field notes is a very Beta activity. You're concentrating, you're up front, you're exceedingly aware of the world around you. But there is an Alpha state that you can shift into, a kind of super-sentience. And after you've done enough of the discipline of field notes, it often happens that you kind of sit back and let all that peripheral stuff filter in. You've been seeing the details, the plants, the animals, the one-two-threes. But you always know there are other things in the air, and when you tune in to them you have moments of tremendous receptivity when time expands.

But when these times come about, you need to write them right then and there. In my field notes there will be very terse entries, bing, bing, bing, bing, and then there will be paragraphs. I mean real sentences, with periods, beginnings, and ends. Almost ninety per cent of the time these paragraphs translate directly into text with just a little cleaning up of syntax — neatening it up and cutting one-third, because I blather a lot. But, yes, indeed, there are such times. And you treasure those times. You are so *thankful* for those times.

NABHAN: That's what you build your essays around, really — those little hot flashes. [laughter] And what is captured in those moments is uncanny. When I did a workshop with Barry Lopez this summer, he said, "Go back and look at your writing in relation to its sound and sense, to see whether the sounds are reinforcing the meaning." And, if you take a journal excerpt from a key moment, it is all in there. I mean you just lift it up, and then you pack around it. And, as Ann said, you do a little bit of trimming, too. But that's what you build around. Sometimes when you've just barely got out of the field the juices are already flowing — like this last winter coming back from Lake Okeechobee after rediscovering a wild gourd that people thought was extinct. I was in the line in the Orlando Airport writing, because the inspiration had started and I saw how all the other pieces fell in right away. And I didn't care whether they fed me anything all the way back to Arizona or not. I wrote nonstop because that one little piece was in place.

ZWINGER: I am profoundly thankful for the modern airplane. It provides some great places to write. It's the white noise. It's the removal — you are physically removed from the Real World. You don't have to answer the telephone. You don't have to talk to anybody.

LUEDERS: You're neither here nor there.

ZWINGER: You're neither here nor there — as in "halfway up the stairs is the stair where I sit." That's where I sometimes do my best writing.

QUESTION: When you start planning a book — like the trip down the Green River and Baja, California — how much do you limit yourself in both time and space to begin with? I mean, what happens? You get this idea and you've got a place, but how much do you limit that space and how much time do you limit yourself to?

ZWINGER: Thank God for deadlines. Otherwise I'd still be writing the Baja book. For that matter, I'd still be writing *Run, River, Run*. Who wants to quit when — what is it? — "time goes so fast when you're having fun"? You need a deadline and a beastly editor who insists that you keep it. I don't really think in terms of limits as far as travel goes — I do all that I can within the framework of available time and money. I hand in a book knowing that I should have done twice as much work, gone to twice as many places, that I need twice as much time, and that I am never going to get any of it. There are ten thousand more adorable facts that nobody cares about but me, and the limits are ones of practicality — of an editor saying, "If you want this book published, it's got to be in *now*." That's not very poetic but it's very practical.

QUESTION: I have a question about your field notes. Wouldn't it be a lot easier to use maybe a tape recorder or a video camera than sketching down on paper—you'd get maybe a more visual idea of what it is—and then take notes at home?

ZWINGER: Number one, if you use a tape recorder, you have to transcribe it, and that is a pain in the tail. I cannot see using a video camera because it tunnels your vision. The one thing you must do is open your vision *out*. You must explore your peripheral vision. Practically, where we go ninety percent of the time you don't have access to a power source or the chance to recharge batteries. Even using a plain camera is detrimental to me. I've tried it. It doesn't work. The only way I can explain it is to say that it so narrows your vision that you miss the rest of what's going on. You're so intent on taking a picture that you miss the javelina that's charging from the rear.

NABHAN: I know some botanists who do running road logs on tapes, but they are really focused on one research problem. Then they just run it up to the next mileage when they're doing a herbarium label. But I think that's real special-case use. Again, even when interviewing Native American people, I don't use a tape recorder for the same reason that I don't have all those reprints on my desk when I write. If it's memorable enough to pass on to others, you probably don't need a tape recorder.

ZWINGER: Nature writing is an old-fashioned profession. Jacob Bronowski was right when he characterized it as "that quaint Victorian profession."

LUEDERS: And it's also a matter of language. For those of us who write, eventually it has to find its form and its expression in the language—in the words and in the verisimilitude that comes through the language. That's a different sort of dimension than you can get from either the sound by itself on the tape recorder or the photograph which reproduces silently and doesn't surround the experience the way language does. It's the gift of language which can reveal the heart of that flash you were talking about earlier, Gary, the "Eureka moment" that makes the essay, the essay that makes the book—and the book makes us all happy we are in this world together. And that's the expression I want to offer on behalf of all of us for the time we've spent with you this evening. Our thanks to you both for coming and engaging in dialogue with us. [applause]

Dialogue Four

NATURAL
HISTORY
AS LITERATURE

Paul Brooks and
Edward Lueders

February 22, 1988

PAUL BROOKS, retired editor-in-chief of Houghton Mifflin Company—mentor of the Peterson's Field Guide Series and publisher of Rachel Carson's *Silent Spring*—now devotes his time to his own writing and conservation causes. His first book, *Roadless Area*, won the John Burroughs Medal. Of his second book, *The Pursuit of Wilderness*, David Brower wrote, "Paul Brooks has earned himself a niche in the hall of fame of wilderness defenders." Among his other books are *The House of Life: Rachel Carson at Work* and *Speaking for Nature: How Literary Naturalists Have Shaped America*.

EDWARD LUEDERS entered the field of natural history writing with *The Clam Lake Papers*. He is an editor of poetry anthologies that contributed much to the poetry in the schools movement, *Reflections on a Gift of Watermelon Pickle*, with Stephen Dunning and Hugh Smith, and *Zero Makes Me Hungry* with Primus St. John. His latest book is a novel, *The Wake of the General Bliss*, and he is at work on a creative nonfiction book, *The Salt Lake Papers*.

LUEDERS: Good evening, and welcome to the last in our series of four dialogues on writing natural history. It's a special pleasure to be sitting here in what appears to be a kind of living room conversation pit with Paul Brooks because we did much the same thing last October in his living room in Lincoln, Massachusetts, where he and his wife, Susan, are stalwarts in the community— New England people, but people who have had world careers in publishing and editing and writing.

Paul Brooks is distinguished as the retired editor-in-chief of Houghton Mifflin Publishers in Boston. His career as an editor has touched the lives and influenced the reading of all of us as well as serving a host of important authors. In particular, I would cite Roger Tory Peterson, whose name graces the Peterson Field Guide Series about which I want to prompt Paul to talk in a few moments. Also Rachel Carson. Paul was her friend and her biographer. I trust all of you are familiar with Rachel Carson's enormously effective and important books, particularly *The Sea Around Us*, which made it possible for her to have a writing career on her own, and *Silent Spring*, the political and ecological ramifications of which are endless. Paul's book *The House of Life: Rachel Carson at Work* is a loving portrait of that lady and her work. Among his other titles are *Roadless Area*, his first book, which won the John Burroughs Medal; *The Pursuit of Wilderness*, which chronicles many of the travels that he and his wife, Susan, have made following out that title in their own lifetime; and a book that tells the basic story of how literary naturalist writing has helped shape America, *Speaking for Nature*.

Paul, I'd like to start our conversation with the beginning, the genesis, and the impact of the Peterson Field Guide Series. It seems to me, as I've considered what's happened since the middle of the century, that one of the most unnoticed, unheralded accomplishments in the whole field of natural history publishing comes from that series of field guides, with Roger Tory Peterson and you at its head, and similar series which have proliferated since.

BROOKS: I think the interesting thing about the Peterson Field Guide influence, in the long run, is not what you necessarily think of first — birds and learning to recognize kinds of birds and so forth — but the fact that this is just the beginning for a lot of people. Unlike more formal science where somebody takes a broad field and then narrows in on one particular aspect of it, with this kind of outdoor nature study, it's more likely that you start by getting enthusiastic about some critter you once never noticed. Suppose you have a Peterson Field Guide and you don't know anything about birds and he shows you how to recognize a red-winged blackbird. Okay, then, the first thing you want to do is to be sure that the swamp in your town where that redwing is nesting is saved. And so these guides lead from one thing to another, from the very specific interest to a general feeling for conservation.

LUEDERS: How many titles in that series now?

BROOKS: It's in the high thirties now. I don't remember exactly.

LUEDERS: And it spread from birds through mammals through flowers?

BROOKS: Yes. And they took a long time and a lot of work. The flower book is a good example. A wonderful woman named Margaret McKenny, who lived in Olympia, started it. That book took twenty-five years in process, and the author, sadly enough, just barely lived to see it published. The problem that Roger and I had in getting these other books going was the fact that, in each case, we were trying to get the top authority — the top herpetologist, the top botanist, the top lepidopterist and so on. And, of course, those were all the busiest people in the trade. It looked sometimes as if these books were never going to get done.

LUEDERS: There is also a popular aspect to them because they appeal so broadly to people who are themselves not specialists but want to have the tools of the specialist, at least for identification, at least for the field work that any of us can do if we have the time and the inclination. And a lot of people now have both.

BROOKS: The way the whole thing started really shows that. Roger Peterson was a young man down in Long Island at the time—he was born in Jamestown, New York—and he used to go out birding with William Vogt, who was a great naturalist himself. Well, Bill Vogt was so impressed with the way this young man could spot these birds, because Roger has such a sharp eye and a sharp ear for the tunes, that he said, "Roger, you've got to get this on paper, and I'll find a publisher for you." Bill Vogt had published books himself. In fact, he did that book *The Road to Survival*, which is one of the earlier conservation books that became a Book of the Month Club selection. He had the entree to the publishers. So Roger outlined this book and did the sample drawings. Vogt took it around to five publishers, four in New York and one in Boston. All of them turned it down. This was in 1933, during the depth of the Depression, and this field guide was a new idea. Fortunately, at Houghton Mifflin we had a gentleman named Francis H. Allen, whose office I shared. He was very nice about having this young sprout from Harvard in his office. He was a very distinguished man who was then chairman of the Massachusetts Audubon Society. We both liked Peterson's book, but while I looked at the manuscript and said, "Oh, sure, this is great; we ought to do it," he had the authority to point out to the management of the place how important it was. So we started in a very small way.

But there is one more story I can tell you about the beginning of this, and then I'll go on to something else. Francis Allen was the chairman of the Massachusetts Audubon Society, but the president was Judge Walcott, a very distinguished, rather formidable character, who was the father of a friend of mine in college. Once when I was there for dinner, I was all excited about this new book. And he asked, "How much is it going to cost?" And I said, "Two dollars and seventy-five cents." He said, "Oh, Paul, you can't sell a bird book for that—just look at these fifty-cent guides." He meant those little Reed Guides that you put in your pocket. And so I subsided. A year later I was back in the same house for dinner. "Paul," he said, "have you heard about this wonderful new guide book that all the ornithologists have in their pockets?" And I said, "Yes, I have." [laughter] And then it went on from there. But now whenever Roger's making a speech and he sees me in the audience, he says, "Well,

when I first went to Houghton Mifflin, I thought Paul Brooks was
the office boy"—which was quite reasonable. We were about the
same age, and I looked like an office boy. But, anyway, that was
where it started and I think, as you suggest, it's done a great deal
for conservation in general.

LUEDERS: The effects are immeasurable, I think. You know, for centuries now, since we're easily into a second century of American
nature writing—a third century if you want to go back to the real
progenitors—there's been a sort of genteel attitude that there's something in the nature essay which smells a little of the library and . . .

BROOKS: Elitist. Yes.

LUEDERS: Exactly. And the Field Guides break through that so effec-
tively, because you take them outdoors with you. They're not housebound. And nature writers are not housebound. Almost the whole
idea behind writing natural history is to get out of the house, even if
that house is your own life, your own self, to project yourself outdoors somehow as a writer. And the reader follows suit. But the
Field Guides do this in practical, actual terms rather than just in
the figurative terms of language. And yet they provide language
and picture together. Now I'm going to ask you about that, because
I know you're an artist of sorts. You do sketches for your own books.
You're frowning, but it's true.

BROOKS: Well, I'm quite limited to sketches. That and Christmas
cards. That's all.

LUEDERS: But you do have that combination. I wonder if there is
something to say about that from your perspective. Roger Peterson
himself is a fine artist. So much of the history of the literature of
natural history is tied to the visual, to the pictorial—through Audubon
back into those writers before photography. And since photography
we have this enormous kind of coffee-table-picture-book approach to
nature, which the photographers have developed. I think of Ansel
Adams, who was a friend of yours, I know, and for whom you
might speak in this respect. Is there a relationship that works for
you, particularly as a publisher and an editor, but also as a reader,

in that combination of the visual, the artist, the photographer and the word, the text?

BROOKS: Well, yes. Let's take somebody like Ansel Adams. He is eloquent in his photography, so to speak. You're right. These approaches can sometimes overlap. Ansel Adams's photographs are not simply nice snapshots of what's there. They are very much in his head just the way, as you say, your writing is in your head. Another kind of example occurs to me. It's a fairly well-known book — at least among the younger generation, I think — a book called *Let Us Now Praise Famous Men* by James Agee and Walker Evans. This seems a far cry from Ansel Adams and Roger Peterson, but in that case we saw just what you're talking about because the photographs were not illustrations of the words. Walker Evans was not illustrating the book; it was a joint venture. It was two people saying the same thing, which happened to be about the southern Appalachians, the sharecropper families and so on. It made a wonderful documentary. And they were both saying the same thing, one in words and one in photographs. So I think, yes, there is that connection.

LUEDERS: And yet I find that the writer of natural history, without neglecting that visual perception, surrounds the experience in the field. We've talked to a number of writers in this series who do this in sensational ways — sensational not in the sense that they "sell," that they are trading on it, but sensational in that all the senses are involved, that there is some sort of round experience when you read them. And the photograph, even though it may be poetic and can be a form of artistic statement upon its subject, is restricted to that plane of the visual on the page. Even though it suggests another dimension, that dimension is not there the way language brings it into our interior experience.

BROOKS: You're very good about some of this in your *Clam Lake Papers*, about sight as the principal sense that we use. And you were talking there about looking at a photograph being a mental exercise, so to speak. I thought, when I was reading that, about one time when Susie and I were in East Africa on safari. We were in what they call the northern frontier district, which is up north of

Nairobi and pretty wild country where they've seen very few white people. We were camped by the only river in about fifty miles — a very, very desert place — and we soon found ourselves surrounded by a very friendly bunch of Rendile natives. They were actually a camel culture and brought their camels up to water every two weeks at this place where we were camped. While we were there, we had with us a few books, including Joy Adamson's *Born Free*, and we showed the pictures to some of these young guys, standing there with their spears and looking over our shoulders. And we were showing a photograph of a lion. At first it didn't mean a thing to them. Then, "Oh, simba, simba!" Of course that's African for lion. They suddenly saw this thing. At first it wasn't a lion. It wasn't anything.

LUEDERS: It was a page.

BROOKS: They weren't used to looking at a photograph. It was a mental process that they weren't prepared for.

LUEDERS: Isn't that curious. It takes a certain mental inclination to see it as a photograph and to reproduce its sense of actuality. And yet how easily we give it our assent and accept the photograph as a testimony, as a document. But the language when people read is another matter. It's a more complex experience — as it is initially a complex experience for the writer himself or herself.

Paul, I'm going to coax you back into the literature of the nineteenth century, for one reason because you are a resident of those areas near Concord, near those New England worthies among our earlier American nature writers. I think particularly of Ralph Waldo Emerson and his neighbor and friend, the younger Henry David Thoreau. *Walden* is a kind of beginning for us all, I guess — a book that we all go back to because it has that combination of motives going for it, even though it is rooted in the fact of Thoreau's being there and observing life day by day at Walden Pond. I'm wondering if you feel any essential difference between those nineteenth-century writers and today's, particularly those that you have dealt with as an editor, but also as a friend and a colleague in your own career. Are they connected?

BROOKS: Well, there's plenty of difference between those particular people you were mentioning. I wouldn't even include Emerson as a nature writer, no. But as for Thoreau, there is a wonderful remark that some Harvard professor made. Thoreau never thought very much of Harvard, but he did, I guess, do fairly well there. One of his professors said some years after Thoreau had graduated, "You know, that young man might have made a good entomologist if he hadn't got under the influence of Emerson." [laughter] There are several other cases like that—careers that might have gone another way. Again at Harvard, somebody remarked when Theodore Roosevelt went there—he was quite interested in natural history, of course—"You know, that man might have become quite a distinguished American naturalist if he hadn't spent so much time on politics." [more laughter] But Teddy's another subject. It's hard to say much about Thoreau in that respect, because he was so much more than a straight naturalist in the modern sense. I think, Ed, I am slowly getting around to answering your question. There is a big difference, certainly, separating most of today's scientific naturalists from somebody like Thoreau. I think he was so much more of a philosopher; but then I'm sure some of the parts of your *Clam Lake Papers* have been compared to Thoreau.

LUEDERS: Well, yes, they have.

BROOKS: That's true, isn't it? Well, then, I've got a very serious question to ask you. Somebody said of Thoreau, "You know, Henry could get more out of ten minutes with a woodchuck than most men could out of a night with Cleopatra." [laughter] Can you say the same?

LUEDERS: I never dated Cleopatra. [more laughter] But I've been known to carry on conversations with marmots that held a lot of pleasure for me.

Actually, it strikes me that there is a combination of things in the work of Henry Thoreau which may come very close to what we find in the best writers of natural history in our time. I'm thinking particularly of Rachel Carson, although certainly she's not alone in this. Others, too, combine the philosophy you're talking about and an associated aesthetic, a feeling of the beauty in nature and its attractiveness to what they unashamedly would have called the soul, with those close observations, which Thoreau also made, of the world around them. So we have the philosophy and the aesthetic and, in a sense, the mythic tied in with natural history — a sense of elevating natural processes somehow into myth. At the same time, there is a sharp perception always, which is scientific, the base of which is naming something — isolating it even, so that it can be known for all of its own characteristics — and then seeing it in the larger circumstances of its ecological setting. These two elements in Thoreau, and in Rachel Carson as well, at least as her career evolved through *Silent Spring*, can then assume a political dimension. The individual author writing as a naturalist somehow moves through that philosophy that most naturalists share and can express into the larger sense of the civilization, into the conduct of society. Certainly Thoreau in *Civil Disobedience* has affected the twentieth century in striking and surprising ways around the globe. So perhaps there's that link I hadn't thought of previously between a Thoreau in the middle of the nineteenth century and a writer such as Rachel Carson in the middle of the twentieth.

BROOKS: Besides the political, I was thinking as you said that of a comment from Thoreau that I mention in *The House of Life* saying that he felt the richer and the better for knowing there was a minnow in the brook. I mean, he always had that feeling of association with other forms of life. And I don't know whether you could really define Thoreau as political. He was just so thoroughly independent that he was going to say what he thought about how the world should be and go to jail if they didn't like it, which he did — overnight.

LUEDERS: Overnight.

BROOKS: That whole jail thing was kind of a pleasant farce, but it did result, as you say, in one of the most effective essays ever written. It inspired Gandhi and Martin Luther King and goodness knows how many other people.

LUEDERS: All of us have been affected directly or indirectly by it, as I trust all of us may become affected, however indirectly, by writers among us right now who, classified loosely, are writing natural history. I emphasize the loosely because it's so hard to classify. There is a category there which is developing somehow, I think, right under our feet, if I can use that figure. Our composite vision as writers of natural history is solidifying somehow into a literary genre without the proponents, the writers themselves, necessarily grouping or feeling themselves already part of a literary group. They're quite individual to this day. I think of Edward Abbey, for instance, whose individualism is Thoreau-esque, being politically and temperamentally turned in much the same way back into the society which he finds himself out of tune with. And yet Abbey's root is in the harsh southwestern landscape, and his affiliation is with that landscape. I think there is a political overtone to virtually all nature writing nowadays because we are becoming educated to the ecological facts of life. We can scarcely escape the conviction that we are in charge of the landscape.

BROOKS: Sure. You could almost make an aphorism out of that. That we destroy anything we don't understand.

LUEDERS: Paul, you trace conservation movements back in *Speaking for Nature* to those beginnings of the National Park System — and to that curious and fortunate confluence of causes in the White House of Theodore Roosevelt at that crucial time.

BROOKS: That gave the nature writers new stature all right.

LUEDERS: It brought the "strenuous life" and "bully" politics of Teddy Roosevelt into an affiliation with writers such as John Burroughs and John Muir at the turn of the century.

BROOKS: It's interesting you mention that because actually I start *Speaking for Nature* with a meeting in, I think, San Francisco, and it must have been about 1911. It was after Roosevelt had returned from the African trip that he took just after his presidency, and he was talking about his experiences but also going into the general theory of what we now call conservation. Incidentally, conservation is a relatively new word, and only in Roosevelt's time did it start to mean what it does now. But anyway, he was speaking about what these writers have done to save the land and to make people understand, and he said, "Writers like John Muir and John Burroughs. . . . " He didn't know it, but both of them were in the audience at the time, which was very appropriate.

Speaking of these connections, do you know what started Burroughs on his nature career? He found a copy of Audubon — the "elephant folio" — in, of all places, the library of West Point Military Academy. He was just a kid then and he got excited about this. Then he started looking at birds himself and getting more and more thrilled by it. Unfortunately, he married a woman who couldn't have cared less and wanted him to go to Wall Street and make some money. But, instead of that, he stayed home at "Slabsides" on the Hudson, and he did well enough in the long run. This is getting way off the point.

LUEDERS: No, it isn't. There isn't any point, anyway; we have so many points to cover. I'm reminded of the poet Walt Whitman and the association of Whitman with nature writers of the late nineteenth century.

BROOKS: Emerson was, of course, the first person to recognize Whitman.

LUEDERS: Yes. And Walt Whitman opens up the door wide to American poets and American literature within the accepted canon — those whom we put in anthologies of American literature without any question that they are central and somehow constitute our lineage. So many of them had associations with those peripheral figures in these anthologies who were nature writers: Burroughs, Muir . . . It's a curious sort of symbiosis, and one of the curiosities for me is that we segregate these writers who were so effective in the national scene — Muir in his way . . .

BROOKS: Oh, yes.

LUEDERS: . . . and Burroughs in his.

BROOKS: Talking about political matters, of course, Muir with Teddy Roosevelt's backing had great influence on our basic conservation policies.

LUEDERS: It may be that their political clout, Muir's particularly, works against their full inclusion in the canon of American literature. I'm not sure that literature in the U.S. isn't somehow supposed to be elite and stand aside from specific political issues.

BROOKS: Yes. You know how Muir got started, by the way?

LUEDERS: In Wisconsin, I know, but beyond that . . . ?

BROOKS: Well, I won't get all the names straight, but, yes, he went to the University of Wisconsin. He came from a pretty poor farm family, as I recall, but he got accepted into the University, among other things, because of his inventiveness. As a young kid, he was very inventive. He produced an alarm clock system. This is getting a little away from nature writing, but he got away from his inventions, too. This was not only an alarm clock but a bed that you slept on, and when the thing went off it threw you out of bed. Well, be that as it may, he apparently could have been quite an inventor and machinist and made a career of that. It was a wife of a professor at Wisconsin, I think named Carr, who got him interested first in flowers and then in other things, and he gradually worked his way out of his machinery and became a naturalist. A lot of these people could have gone in several directions early in their lives.

LUEDERS: I think of another connection with Wisconsin, Aldo Leopold . . .

BROOKS: Oh, yes.

LUEDERS: . . . who now is widely anthologized and among us in print in many single pieces as well as in his *Sand County Almanac*, which is out in a new edition, incidentally. That Wisconsin connection is a good one for me, as you might imagine, since I grew up in Chicago and, as the bumper stickers have it, escaped to Wisconsin every chance I got. There is still a part of me that is up there around Clam Lake in what I'm afraid I called "the pine woods." I'm afraid of that because I got a response from a reader in Maine who is a forester and said he enjoyed the book but he was quite sure most of those pines were firs. [laughter]

BROOKS: Well, mentioning the connection of Maine, a classic book there is Sarah Orne Jewett's *The Country of the Pointed Firs*. They were spruce. [more laughter]

LUEDERS: Poetic license is what I claim. I wonder what she would call it.

BROOKS: Speaking of Leopold, I think it's interesting the way he developed. He was quite a sportsman, as of course you know—liked hunting and so on—and his specialty was game management. It wasn't necessarily nature in the sense that we think of it. And if you look back on it, it turns out that almost all the early conservationists began as hunters. George Bird Grinnell, who was a member of the original Boone and Crockett Club, the hunters' club that Theodore Roosevelt belonged to, was responsible in the long run for creating Glacier Park. He knew that country and he'd been hunting up there and he saved it. Enos Mills may not have been a sportsman—I don't know—but he singlehandedly created Rocky Mountain Park. Up until almost our time, the people who were the leading conservationists started as hunters, and my feeling is that they all finally grew up. But there is a little contradiction in that, I realize.

The Audubon Society itself started in the middle of a sportsmen's magazine, not *Field and Stream* but one called *Forest and Stream*. This same man, George Bird Grinnell, was the editor of it, and he started a little sort of club, mainly for children, to interest them in birds. This grew and grew until finally it began to overwhelm him and he had to let it go. Then it was out for a while and then it was started up again. But I think I'm right in saying that his original plan involved thinking up a name for this organization. Well, he had been to the Audubon place in upstate New York and he had known Lucy Audubon, the widow, and he thought it would be a good name for the society. So that's how it got to be the Audubon Society.

LUEDERS: You have been active in the societies, including the Sierra Club. I wonder if you have some perspective on the relationship, which is perhaps an obvious one, and perhaps in some ways not so obvious, between the organizations and the authors. Is it just in our own time, very recently, that the Sierra Club publications, for instance, have done so much, republishing your *Speaking for Nature*,

for instance, and keeping that sort of writing before us? Or does it
go back farther than this? I know the connection with Muir, but
beyond that?

BROOKS: No I don't think it does go back. I think it's very recent.
The prominent Sierra Club publications program really started under
Dave Brower, who is a very dynamic entrepreneur. He started with
those exhibit format books. And you were speaking of Ansel Adams —
the first of his books was not one of the color ones; it was black and
white, because that's what Ansel did. That started off a whole series,
and by that time the club was into publishing, so to speak. I was
chairman of their publishing committee for quite a long time, and
they really did very well with these big books until they started to
be imitated by other publishers. And then they went on to diversify
and do more general things. All those organizations now, of course,
are putting out very attractive and very effective magazines. I don't
think this applies so much to books, but of course, *Audubon* — the
National Audubon magazine — is a superb thing, and was always
famous for its photographs. But a few years ago — I think this is
really surprising — it got the Magazine Publishers Association award
for its articles, quite aside from all those fantastically beautiful pictures. So there you have a society that does just exactly what you
were asking about.

LUEDERS: That's right, and I think of the rest of the magazines
which have proliferated and established themselves now within the
whole field of magazine publishing as semipopular journals in which
scientists write for a broad audience, the generally educated audience . . .

BROOKS: And regular contributors in natural history magazines —
Stephen Jay Gould, for example. He's a wonderful writer.

LUEDERS: . . . and the public connections there and elsewhere with
natural history field work that museums as well as conservation
societies and other groups are sponsoring. There is something alive
in this whole field that links in with all the writers we've been talking about — the writers you've dealt with — the writers since Rachel
Carson and Loren Eiseley. Those two seem to me to be sitting
somehow there over our shoulders as we write in the eighties. Back

in the 1940s and 50s they both established this union of poetic insight and scientific observation with the gift of language that brings these somehow incandescently through their pages to the reader. Rachel Carson, by the way, was a trained marine biologist, was she not?

BROOKS: She was the first woman, other than secretaries, ever employed by the U.S. Fish and Wildlife Service. It was then the Bureau of Fisheries. And it's interesting you mentioned that business of your response because she said somewhere in one of her books, "I am not ashamed of my emotional response." I think this was as she was watching that herring run, a wonderful sight. She was never sentimental, but she was not afraid of being considered emotional.

LUEDERS: Never sentimental?

BROOKS: Certainly not — about the most unsentimental woman I've ever known.

LUEDERS: Tell us more about her as a person, as a writer, the combination that you knew.

BROOKS: Personally she was very understated. One time I called her long-distance to tell her that *Silent Spring* was a choice of the Book of the Month Club. She simply said, "Oh, Paul, that's very nice," and then went on to talk about something else. And she had — I hate to make such a bald statement — I think she had no small talk. At the Book of the Month Club luncheon she was sitting next to Harry Sherman, the president of the club, and looking up the table you saw these two people sitting next to each other in complete silence, without any communication at all. She put most of the energies and qualities you're talking about into her writing. When you got to know her, of course, it was a very different thing. But to the public as a whole she looked like a very quiet, very unobtrusive, very understated person.

LUEDERS: But she was a poet on the page.

BROOKS: Oh, yes. Also, her books were an example in a way of what makes books sell. Her first book, called *Under the Sea Wind*, published by Simon and Schuster, came out just before the war started, just two weeks before Pearl Harbor, which wasn't a very good time to have a book published. Anyway—I happened to look it up—it sold, I think, 1,650 copies altogether. It was a complete flop. Then exactly ten years later, she published with the Oxford Press *The Sea Around Us*, which became one of the best sellers of all time. And that same year, 1951, Oxford bought the rights for the earlier book, reprinted *Under the Sea Wind*, which had been a failure, and it instantly sold sixty thousand copies, because it had this successful author's name, and it kept going.

LUEDERS: Of course that sort of story is a point of despair to a good many of us writers who don't have the names. And that, Paul, leads me to a question about publishing which makes me sound like one of my students asking me—and now I'm asking you because of your long and illustrious career . . .

BROOKS: Where does that put me—at the head of the food chain? [laughter]

LUEDERS: I'm going to use that awful word "market," awful because it seems so far from the field in which the naturalist writer does the work that turns into the page that turns into the book. Do you sense any change over the years you've been in publishing in the market for natural history writing, and would you have any advice for people who are inclined to write natural history in our own time—looking ahead toward the future audience for it?

BROOKS: I don't think you could see that much change in a few decades. The only change, I think, is the obvious one of quite a steady growth. For instance, the first printing of the Peterson Field Guide was, I think, two thousand copies. It's now, of course, over a million. But there is a growing natural history literate audience. I suppose that's really what we're talking about. And they've been coming to it for all sorts of reasons. I mean, for instance, for the museum programs and all these various trips now that are advertised all over the world. I haven't thought of this particular idea before, but I'm sure all these, like the Lindblad trips that take people all over, cater to people who are going to end up by reading natural history books and being interested in the whole field, although they might never have had the slightest inclination before they left.

LUEDERS: It's interesting that *terra incognita* is largely gone. Lindblad and the other specialists will take you anywhere and drop you down with a helicopter, and there you are in a landscape that was mental for you before, experienced only through books and perhaps drawings, perhaps photographs.

BROOKS: It's kind of a worry in a way. I argued with Roger Peterson about this a little bit, because he, of course, was Lindblad's great strength, as he was hired to go on these various trips. And it gave Roger a wonderful chance to see all those places that he never would have seen otherwise and also to be lionized by many attractive people. But I said, "How about Lindblad opening up all these last places that could have been sort of kept untouched?" Roger had, I guess, a convincing answer to that. He said, "Those are going to be opened up anyway, and Lindblad is doing it the right way"—implication: thanks to what I, Roger, am doing in teaching these people to respect the wildlife.

LUEDERS: It's the difference between education and exploitation of the globe.

BROOKS: Yes. And so I think he's probably right that you can't keep places pristine. Years ago, before your time, there was a book by John Buchan called *The Last Secrets*. Did you ever read that book?

LUEDERS: I don't know that one.

BROOKS: There were about twelve chapters on various places that had never been explored, including Mount Everest, of course. But I bet there are none of those twelve secrets left.

LUEDERS: I'm reminded of the title of your first book, *Roadless Area*, and think of the maps which are now filled in with roads in those open spaces, even if they are dotted lines, so that people go there. And the four-wheel drives and the off-road vehicles are covering the earth the way Sherwin-Williams paint used to in their ads.

BROOKS: Incidentally, did you know where that title, *Roadless Area*, comes from? It's a technical term of the Forest Service. The first roadless area was the canoe country — the Quetico canoe country, which is my wife's and my favorite of all places. We took many, many canoe trips there and across the border into Canada. And that was officially known as a roadless area, just like a wilderness area. And now there are roadless areas, I think, throughout the Forest Service in different places. But that's where I got it. I didn't invent the term.

LUEDERS: You know, what we're investigating here is travel literature. There is an affinity of natural history writing with travel literature, with that sense of going somewhere with notebook — perhaps with camera, but with a naturalist's eye at work — going where people normally do not go, or most people are unable to go. But there is an increasing encroachment now on all these areas and perhaps this alliance between travel literature and natural history writing is running its course. I think of Barry Lopez's book on the Arctic. Now he's been to the Antarctic, too. He is able to put in his vivid language and his kind of soaring view of the natural world these places which have been impossible for us, until now, to suppose we as individuals might visit. This remote world is diminishing, but I don't know that the writing diminishes. It seems to me that we become more aware of the whole globe and our role in it when we see more of it. The experience of jet travel adds a lot. You and I are old enough so that we can think back to those early airplanes that flew barely into the atmosphere. Now we are so far above the terrain that we see the globe and the curvature and the pollution and other Earth elements which previously have been thrust into the imagination rather than actual experience for those of us who are not explorers, are not those nineteenth-century adventurers who perished trying to get those remote places somehow on the map.

BROOKS: Of course that was the extreme case with the early astronauts. Archie MacLeish had an awfully good poem about that when we made the first landing on the moon, dealing with the fact that you are up there and looking at this little ball and realizing that's all you've got and you'd better take care of it.

LUEDERS: You know, that returns me to this element of philosophical insight in natural history writing which I think waxes with some of the writers and is secondary with others, and perhaps needs to be modulated with that fine tuning that a good writer is capable of. I mean that moving toward myth, that moving of the scientific fact and observation to the larger implications—the sort of thing that Loren Eiseley, as a poet, did with his anthropological perspectives, with the training that he had as a scientist, with that possibility of seeing things individually and yet finding them a part of a larger whole than we can encompass with our simple human vision. There is something moving toward reverence among many of these writers.

BROOKS: Oh, yes.

LUEDERS: Certainly awe. Delight. Joy. All of these surprisingly affirmative attitudes in a time when so much is negative. So much in writing, so much in the fiction and the poetry of our time is narrowed down and circumscribed by some sort of individual vision, which is a closed circle. And the large circle of the globe—the sphere rather than the circle, if you will— is something that we now have in that image of us from outer space. I've forgotten which astronaut is involved here. Isn't that nice that I don't have to attribute this to one because I'm sure it is speaking for everyone who has seen those photographs. And we're back to the possibility of the photograph and the visual here. I'm referring to the image of the Earth seen from space and that aesthetic response that one of the astronauts, looking down for the first time, felt compelled to say, speaking of beauty rather than fixing that moment in some predisposed saying—like Neil Armstrong's—what is it?—"One small step for man, one giant step for mankind." He was sexist in that one, I guess, wasn't he?

BROOKS: At least he didn't say personkind. [laughter]

LUEDERS: Maybe you can attribute this to the particular astronaut who spoke it, who said with awe, and I think with reverence, "The Earth is beautiful." As if this weren't possible to say from where we stand upon it. But that's what writers of natural history have been saying in their own way for decades, for centuries, for generations — ever since there has been such a thing as natural history to be written.

BROOKS: Incidentally, in your first of this series, I think you had one person here, E. O. Wilson of Harvard, who has very much this view. I guess he read from some of his *Biophilia*, didn't he?

LUEDERS: Yes, he did.

BROOKS: And he has that wonderful combination.

LUEDERS: There is a remarkable actual union of these elements in natural history. I find it in writer after writer, each one individualizing it, each one somehow speaking a piece which says, as Barry Lopez put it, "I'm concerned with something larger than my own view of what I see, but I see what I see as sharply as I am able."

Do you have any prospects for natural history writing, Paul? Do you have any sense of where it's going?

BROOKS: I hadn't thought of that. I was wondering whether, now you mention it, there might be a reversal of this trend, that maybe there is so much being covered that natural history writers are going to start getting more specialized. A hard thought, I think, but I don't know. I don't know particularly where it's going, and I don't see any clear trends. I'm on the board of judges for the Burroughs Medal, and we get a number of books every year; but they are a complete scatteration of things from very broad subjects to very concentrated near-home-to-the-author subjects.

One thing I've noticed, looking over those books that come in, is that more and more are being done by small, sometimes new, publishers. There are growing numbers of small publishers, local publishers all over the country, more in the west than in the east. What this means, maybe, is that the larger publishers feel they have to have bigger, quicker sales, and most of these books are not all that saleable. But it's interesting to see how many darn good small publishers there are in this field now.

LUEDERS: That's important to the diversity of books in our lives, and it strikes me that diversity is one of the notes that natural history writing is presenting to us. As I said earlier, it's so hard to classify. My experience with *The Clam Lake Papers* may be a case in point. Nobody knows where to shelve it. [laughter]

BROOKS: Good, so you won't become stale. They can't put you on the shelf, they have to have you hanging around all the time. [more laughter] That's great.

LUEDERS: It may be that the small publishers don't have to worry about that neat classification, about finding that niche which has already been filled successfully so that this book will be successful simply because it falls in that niche.

BROOKS: That is a very good point. I can remember that from my publishing days. You present this great new book to the salesmen and they say, "Yeah, but how do we tell the bookseller where he puts this?"—what shelf is it on, what section?

LUEDERS: This may mirror something that Edward O. Wilson said to us in his dialogue with Barry Lopez at the beginning of this series. E. O. Wilson, of course, stands for diversity in the genetic pool. And adapting that to our concerns, it seems to me that the diversity in what the writer of natural history has as his subject, which is endless, bottomless, and topless as well, is somehow built in along with the fact that an individual author registering himself or herself on the page for readers can also draw upon the diversity of individualism in our society. And what you have here is something that deals in facts but still does not classify—because it eventually can cover everything. It has that potential more fully than the camera, to return to that subject. We feel photographs are real because eventually, I suppose, you could photograph everything. Ah, but you can't. You cannot photograph human experience and that observation which is a human observation. The only tool we have for that is the language which is common among us.

BROOKS: It's the same reason that a great portrait is truer than a photograph.

LUEDERS: Shall we invite questions from the audience, Paul? They may lead us in some directions which we haven't taken ourselves.

BROOKS: I think that's a first-rate idea.

QUESTION: This is sort of a literary question. Can you speak of the influence of natural history writing in this century and the last, I suppose, on the trend in fiction that's commonly called "naturalism"— and if you see that as a dead trend?

LUEDERS: Paul is pointing to Professor Lueders to respond to this one. [laughter] The question is the relationship, if any, of natural history writing to what at the turn of the century was called literary naturalism—what is still called, to this day, literary naturalism.

The curious link came by way of Darwinian evolutionary thought and what developed into Social Darwinism. And the curious oppositions that I find in this are interesting to me because the literary naturalists of the turn of the century, authors such as Theodore Dreiser, Emile Zola, Stephen Crane, Jack London, and their ilk, were writing out of a philosophy which supposed the utter indifference of the universe to the wishes of the individual human being. This was a kind of depressing antidote to the romanticism that preceded it in the nineteenth century—and to all idealized romantic thought, generally speaking. It was documentary in its approach, because it didn't want emotional responses which were not natural within their setting. But, generally, it was a downer.

Even with the advent of Henry Adams, that polymath at the turn of the century who was a student of more scientific subjects and more subjects within the humanities than perhaps any previous American author, the tone was ironic and pessimistic. He was a historian by profession whose autobiography, *The Education of Henry Adams*, in the early decades of our century, made light of the fact that he never was educated, that he never answered the basic questions, and that he was overcome by the developments in science, particularly those which seemed to dissolve, to lose ground—entropy and the principles of degeneration that were built into radium and the discoveries of X rays and so forth.

BROOKS: . . . and acceleration.

LUEDERS: Yes. All of this reflected a profound sense of desolation and cosmic indifference, which found its modern poetic equivalent in T. S. Eliot's *The Waste Land*. And yet I find in the natural history writers, whether they are the nineteenth-century ones or the twentieth-century ones, the central continuity is somehow this element of delight.

BROOKS: But, speaking of Henry Adams, you remember his remarks about how Harvard had nothing to teach him, but Agassiz's lectures were the one thing that he thought were great. Agassiz, in this case, lectured mainly on geology, being, along with John Muir, one of the two people who really founded the whole glacial theory. This is interesting because you don't think of Henry Adams as a person particularly interested in natural history.

LUEDERS: No. But his friendship with Clarence King, for instance . . .

BROOKS: Oh, Clarence King! He is a wonderful guy . . .

LUEDERS: A wonderful nineteenth-century figure.

BROOKS: I could get going on Clarence King.

LUEDERS: See what you've launched us into here — the connections between science and literature, science and the humanities, in these figures. This question raises all of these attitudinal matters which, for me, lead to this curious fact that the literary naturalists seem to be depressed about life in general. At best, they're indifferent, whereas writers of natural history, writing outside of themselves into the world of nature, are full of affirmation of one order or another, just as the best science, it seems to me, has a rule of affirmation behind it rather than of negation.

QUESTION: What role do you think gender has in the writing of natural history? Do you see a difference in terms of the female voice versus the masculine?

BROOKS: You want me to take that one?

LUEDERS: Please do.

BROOKS: Well, one thing is that natural history writing by women is fairly new. I always cherished the remark of an early natural history writer named Wilson Flagg who wrote for some New England magazine. He was talking about how it was quite suitable for women to study flowers, "but a lady could not, without a certain eccentricity, follow birds or quadrupeds into the woods." [laughter] Well, there were certain women who were reasonably eccentric enough to do that. But, at the beginning of the whole interest in birds, women writers were very important. One of them, Mabel Osgood Wright, was the founder of one of the first bird sanctuaries. A wonderful woman named Florence Merriam really got out in the roughest places with men, and she wrote a book called *A-Birding on a Bronco*. And this interest gradually built up. Now is your question really whether I see any difference right now between women's writing on natural history and men's?

QUESTIONER: When you look at Mary Austin and Rachel Carson and Annie Dillard . . .

BROOKS: I don't think the sense of gender comes in much at all. Of course, they were very different people. Mary Austin was very aggressive, very strong and highly political, of course — trying to save California. Well, what you might be asking is this: if an unidentified manuscript came in, could I tell whether it was by a man or woman? No, probably not.

LUEDERS: I think there is a highly individual note that may have something to do with the gender, but on the page I'm not sure that's what gets top billing in natural history writing — or should. That's a political statement, I realize, but it's also a literary statement. We have women authors in all fields, and some of them are more clearly writing from a woman's point of view than others. But I think this is just as true of men authors. Some of them are more clearly masculine in their projection of themselves on the page than others. The fact that there is an imbalance on the shelves and in the halls of the publishers is another matter, and this is also political, I realize. But I don't think it comes back to say, necessarily, that you have a different role of authorship in natural history depending on whether it is a woman or a man writing. The potential for the woman's point of view, on the other hand, is still to be developed, just as the potential for the man's point of view is still to be developed. We haven't written all the books on natural history, have we? There are still authors among us—I'd like to think, in this audience, for instance—who will be writing out of their own experience; and, if that experience is heavily on the side of the gender, then this will be reflected in their writing.

BROOKS: Some of the early ones like Gene Stratton Porter, who was somewhat of a sentimental writer and was enormously successful, were women who were writing for women. But I wouldn't apply that to the women who are writing on nature today.

QUESTION: How would you classify the literature of the earliest explorers and discoverers, the Europeans who came to the New World with that sense of wonder? We get a good many natural wonders in their writing, but it wasn't natural history in your sense, was it? And is there a continuity between their time and ours?

LUEDERS: Well, I guess Captain John Smith sold pretty well.

BROOKS: He was a wonderful advertising man.

LUEDERS: That's right. He was a real-estate-promotion-advertising man. And there were the fabulous stories of Spanish exploration in the southwest. But I'm thinking of the descriptions which went back with Smith and others from Virginia and from the eastern coastline and from the Caribbean area. Yes, I think, after its fashion, if we put it in the time and place, there is an element of the natural history writer there, although these were not people trained in our sense scientifically, for the most part. They did, however, send artists on many of these voyages, artists to make visual as well as linguistic the reports that came back. There is in their work that post-Renaissance sense of the natural world yet to be discovered—recording the wonders of the world which could be described to people back home. This may be associated, it seems to me, in the same way as we were speaking earlier of these excursions into little-known areas—not only the nineteenth-century explorers looking for previously unexplored and unexperienced parts of the globe, but those of us who do it today and come back with our photo albums or, if we are at all literary, our notebooks full of what we've seen.

BROOKS: Some of those early explorers still make fascinating reading. I was thinking that one of my childhood favorite books was Nansen's *Farthest North*. This was, of course, before anybody had gotten to the North Pole . . .

LUEDERS: You *do* go back a long way. [laughter]

BROOKS: Look, my dear man, [more laughter] this book was written before I was born, but I think the North Pole was discovered in the same year—so . . . When was the North Pole discovered?

LUEDERS: This is your speech, not mine.

BROOKS: You brought the subject up, now, come on.

LUEDERS: Does anyone in the house know when the North Pole was discovered? Is it still disputed?

BROOKS: Well, it was Peary, wasn't it? I don't think Cook . . . Has Cook still got a following? [laughter] Well, I thought it was discovered in 1909, but maybe not. Anyway, I was. [more laughter; applause]

LUEDERS: Actually, dear Paul, that is very much to the point. Because your longevity, your wit, your presence, your illustrious career, the way in which you have served all of us as well as individual authors through a long period of a very fruitful life is very much to the point of our being in your distinguished company tonight and having you as our guest on this last of the series. You can hear the mounting finale here. You can surely recognize a coda when you hear one. I want to say it is my particular delight that you accepted our invitation to be a collaborator in this series. You have graced it most personably and memorably this evening. Your versatile career as an editor, publisher, biographer, historian, and author has added length and breadth to this concluding dialogue on the writing of natural history. [sustained applause]

FURTHER READINGS FROM THE AUTHORS

BARRY LOPEZ

Books:

Crossing Open Ground. Charles Scribner's Sons, 1988.

Arctic Dreams. Charles Scribner's Sons, 1986.

Winter Count. Charles Scribner's Sons, 1981.

Of Wolves and Men. Charles Scribner's Sons, 1978.

River Notes. Andrews & McMeel, 1979.

Giving Birth to Thunder. Andrews & McMeel, 1978.

Desert Notes. Andrews & McMeel, 1976.

Selected Essays:

"The American Geographies," in *The Goodwill Games Book: Soviet and American Essays,* University of Washington Press, 1989.

"A Chinese Garland," *North American Review,* September 1988.

"Informed by Indifference: A Walk in Antarctica," *Harper's,* May 1988.

"Landscapes Open and Closed: A Journey through South Africa," *Harper's,* July 1987.

"Japan's True North," *New York Times Magazine,* pt. 2, "The Sophisticated Traveler," October 5, 1986.

EDWARD O. WILSON

Books:

Biodiversity, editor. National Academy Press, 1988.

Biophilia. Harvard University Press, 1984.

Promethean Fire: Reflections on the Origin of Mind, with Charles J. Lumsden. Harvard University Press, 1983.

Genes, Mind, and Culture, with Charles J. Lumsden. Harvard University Press, 1981.

Caste and Ecology in the Social Insects, with George F. Oster. Princeton University Press, 1978.

On Human Nature. Harvard University Press, 1978.

Sociobiology: The New Synthesis. Harvard University Press, 1975.

Ecology, Evolution, and Population Biology, editor. Harvard University Press, 1974.

The Insect Societies. Harvard University Press, 1971.

The Theory of Island Biogeography, with R. H. MacArthur. Princeton University Press, 1967.

Selected Essays:

"The Diversity of Life," *in* Harm J. de Blij, editor, *Earth '88: Changing Geographic Perspectives* (Proceedings of the Centennial Symposium), National Geographic Society, 1988.

"The Causes of Ecological Success: The Case of the Ants," (The Sixth Tansley Lecture, Oxford University), *Journal of Animal Ecology,* 1985.

"Storm over the Amazon," *in* Daniel Halpern, editor, *Antaeus,* Autumn 1986, The Ecco Press.

"The Biological Diversity Crisis: A Challenge to Science," *Issues in Science and Technology,* Fall 1985.

"In the Queendom of the Ants: A Brief Autobiography," *in* Donald A. Dewsbury, editor, *Leaders in the Study of Animal Behavior: Autobiographical Perspectives,* Bucknell University Press, 1985.

"The Conservation of Life," *Harvard Magazine,* May 1974.

ROBERT FINCH

Books:

The Norton Book of Nature Writing, edited with John Elder. W. W. Norton, scheduled for Spring 1990.

Outlands: Journeys to the Outer Edges of Cape Cod. David R. Godine, 1986.

The Primal Place. W. W. Norton, 1983.

Common Ground: A Naturalist's Cape Cod. David R. Godine, 1981.

Selected Essays:

"Introduction" to Henry Beston's *The Outermost House,* Viking Penguin, 1988.

"Into the Maze" and "Scratching," *in* Stephen Trimble, editor, *Words from the Land: Encounters with Natural History Writing,* Peregrine Smith, 1988.

"Introduction" to Aldo Leopold's *Sand County Almanac,* Oxford University Press, 1987.

"Introduction" to Henry Thoreau's *Cape Cod,* Parnassus Imprints, 1984.

TERRY TEMPEST WILLIAMS

Books:

Refuge. Viking, scheduled for Spring 1990.

Coyote's Canyon, photographs by John Telford. Peregrine Smith, 1989.

Earthly Messengers. Western Slope Press, 1989.

Between Cattails. Charles Scribner's Sons, 1985.

Pieces of White Shell: A Journey to Navajoland. Charles Scribner's Sons, 1984.

The Secret Language of Snow, with Ted Major. Sierra Club Books, 1984.

Selected Essays:

"Pink Flamingos," *Northern Lights,* Spring 1989.

"A Naturalist's Notebook," *Deseret News* (Salt Lake City), weekly column, 1984–1986.

"The Canyon's Edge," Canyonlands Field Institute, narration for multimedia presentation, 1988.

"The Bowl," *North American Review,* Winter 1988.

"In the Country of Grasses: A Great Basin Naturalist in the Serengeti," *VII Magazine* (Salt Lake City), September 1987.

"Kokopelli's Return," *Backpacker,* July 1987.

GARY PAUL NABHAN

Books:

Enduring Seeds: Native American Agriculture and Wild Plant Conservation. North Point, 1989.

Saguaro: A View of Saguaro National Monument and the Tucson Basin. Southwest Parks and Monuments Association, 1986.

Gathering the Desert. University of Arizona Press, 1985.

The Desert Smells Like Rain: A Naturalist in Papago Indian Country. North Point, 1982.

Selected Essays:

"Where Has All the Panic Gone?" and "Where the Birds Are Our Friends: A Tale of Two Oases," *in* Stephen Trimble, editor, *Words from the Land: Encounters with Natural History Writing,* Peregrine Smith, 1988.

"Comments on Literature and Landscape," *in* Cynthia Farah, editor, *Literature and Landscape,* Texas Western Press, 1988.

"The Sonoran Desert," *in* Tom Miller, editor, *The Land and the People,* University of Arizona Press, 1986.

"Wild Desert Relatives of Crops: Their Direct Uses as Food," with R. S. Felger, *in* G. E. Wickems, J. R. Goodin, and D. V. Fields, editors, *Plants for Arid Lands,* London: George Allen and Unwin, 1985.

"Replenishing Desert Agriculture with Native Plants and Their Desert Symbionts," *in* W. Jackson, W. Berry, and B. Colman, editors, *Meeting the Expectations of the Land,* North Point, 1984.

ANN HAYMOND ZWINGER

Books:

These Mysterious Lands: The Four Deserts of the United States. E. P. Dutton, 1989.

John Xanthus: The Fort Tejon Letters (1857–1859). University of Arizona Press, 1986.

A Desert Country near the Sea: The Cape Country of Baja California. Harper & Row, 1983; paperback, University of Arizona Press, 1987.

A Conscious Stillness: Two Naturalists on Thoreau's Rivers, with Edwin Way Teale. Harper & Row, 1982; paperback, University of Massachusetts Press, 1984.

Wind in the Rock: The Canyonlands of Southeastern Utah. Harper & Row, 1978; paperback, University of Arizona Press, 1986.

Run, River, Run: A Naturalist's Journey down One of the Great Rivers of the West. Harper & Row, 1975; paperback, University of Arizona Press, 1984.

Land above the Trees: A Guide to American Alpine Tundra, with Dr. Beatrice E. Willard. Harper & Row, 1971; paperback, 1986.

Beyond the Aspen Grove. Random House, 1970; paperback, University of Arizona Press, 1986.

Selected Essays:

"Of Desert Rivers and Pipistrelles," *Audubon,* May 1989.

"Drawing from Experience," *Orion,* Winter 1987.

"A World of Infinite Variety," *Antaeus,* Autumn 1986.

"The Art of Wandering," *Orion,* January 1986.

"A Hungarian in Baja," *Audubon,* January 1985.

"Becoming Mom to a Word Processor," *Smithsonian,* February 1982.

PAUL BROOKS

Books:

Two Park Street: A Publishing Memoir. Houghton Mifflin, 1986.

The Old Manse. Houghton Mifflin, 1983.

Speaking for Nature: How Literary Naturalists from Henry Thoreau to Rachel Carson Have Shaped America. Sierra Club Books, 1983.

The View from Lincoln Hill. Houghton Mifflin, 1976.

The House of Life: Rachel Carson at Work. Houghton Mifflin, 1973.

The Pursuit of Wilderness. Houghton Mifflin, 1971.

Roadless Area. Alfred A. Knopf, 1964.

Selected Essays:

"Superjetport or Everglades Park," *Audubon,* July 1969.

"A Plot to Drown Alaska," *in* Gerald Walker, editor, *Best Magazine Articles,* Crown Press, 1966.

"The Golden Plains of Tanganyika," *Horizon,* Winter 1965.

EDWARD LUEDERS

Books:

The Wake of the General Bliss. University of Utah Press, 1989.

The Clam Lake Papers: A Winter in the North Woods. Harper & Row, 1977; paperback, Abingdon Festival Books, 1983.

Zero Makes Me Hungry & Other Poems for Today, edited with Primus St. John. Scott, Foresman, 1976.

Some Haystacks Don't Even Have Any Needle & Other Complete Poems, edited with Stephen Dunning and Hugh Smith. Scott, Foresman, 1969.

Reflections on a Gift of Watermelon Pickle & Other Modern Verse, edited with Stephen Dunning and Hugh Smith. Scott, Foresman, 1966.

Carl Van Vechten. Twayne United States Authors Series, 1965.

The College and Adult Reading List of Books in Literature and the Fine Arts, editor. NCTE/Washington Square Press, 1962.

Carl Van Vechten & the Twenties. University of New Mexico Press, 1955.

Selected Essays:

"Beyond Specialization: Writing for Readers," *National Forum, The Phi Kappa Phi Journal,* Spring 1989.

"The Human Animal: Instinct with Language," *Utah English Journal,* 1987.

"Harlan Hubbard's *Payne Hollow:* Life on the Fringe of Society," *Rocky Mountain Review of Language & Literature,* Autumn 1975.

"Color Symbolism in the Songs of the American Indian," *Western Humanities Review,* Spring 1958.